Peyote
Dreams

"Brilliantly and poetically written, completely engrossing, and magically able to describe the indescribable—the majesty and inner drama of the peyote journey—Duits's work is reminiscent of (but maybe even richer and more evocative than) Huxley's writings on his own mescaline journeys."

ROSS HEAVEN, AUTHOR OF *CACTUS OF MYSTERY* AND
SHAMANIC QUEST FOR THE SPIRIT OF SALVIA

Peyote
Dreams

Journeys in
the Land of Illumination

CHARLES DUITS

Translated by Zara De Yazd

Park Street Press
Rochester, Vermont • Toronto, Canada

Park Street Press
One Park Street
Rochester, Vermont 05767
www.ParkStPress.com

Text stock is SFI certified

Park Street Press is a division of Inner Traditions International

Originally published in French under the title *Le pays de l'éclairement* by Éditions Denoël, Paris

Library of Congress Cataloging-in-Publication Data
Duits, Charles. 1925–1991
  [Pays de l'éclairement. English]
  Peyote dreams : journeys in the land of illumination / Charles Duits ; translated by Zara De Yazd.
     p. ; cm.
  Includes bibliographical references and index.
  Summary: "A detailed account of the transformation of consciousness and discovery of life's purpose brought on by peyote.—Provided by publisher.
  Originally published in French under the title *L'Pays de l'éclairement* by Éditions Denoël, Paris, c1967.
  ISBN 978-1-59477-449-2 (pbk.) — ISBN 978-1-62055-160-8 (e-book)
  I. Title.
  [DNLM: 1. Mescaline—Personal Narratives. 2. Hallucinations—chemically induced—Personal Narratives. QV 77.7]
  RM666.P48
  616.86'340092—dc23
                                                                2013014486

Printed and bound in the United States by Lake Book Manufacturing, Inc. The text stock is SFI certified. The Sustainable Forestry Initiative® program promotes sustainable forest management.

10 9 8 7 6 5 4 3 2 1

Text design and layout by Brian Boynton
This book was typeset in Garamond Premier Pro with Serif Gothic as a display typeface

CONTENTS

This poison shall remain
in all our veins even when,
the fanfare turning,
we shall be restored to the old disharmony.

"Morning of Drunkenness,"
in *Illuminations*, Arthur Rimbaud

INTRODUCTION

He comes down, wakes up, on the other side of the dream.
VICTOR HUGO

Western consciousness instinctively adopts a hostile attitude when confronted with sacramental plants.

It views those who use them, sincere as their intentions may be, as lawbreakers and delinquents. It even refuses to accept that these plants have occupied an important place in the religious life of certain civilizations and still hold one in that of the Native Americans.

This refusal, and the discomfort of which it is a sign, primarily derives, as we shall see, *from the image the West has constructed of man's relationship with the universe.*

This is because we never cast doubt—although it is we who have made doubt the foundation of our philosophical tradition—on the exactitude of that image, for which reason the use of sacramental plants scares and scandalizes us.

It seems obvious to us that every substance that acts on the mind—the word we use to designate, in fact, the sole form of intelligence—is an obfuscator, a "narcotic." Therefore, the protests

1

raised by their adepts have no power. If sacramental plants fog the crystal of sight, they should be banned, and the attitude of the authorities is justified, but what if their effect is entirely different? No one envisions that possibility. The implications would be too serious.

However, it has become essential to envision this. For some years now, new substances have been invented—mescaline, LSD—that are currently enjoying vast dissemination. Many, especially among the young, are the explorers of the Oneirocosmos,* and the books dedicated to their adventures are plentiful.

Suspicion continues, however, to surround those who make use of what I would like to call, in order to distinguish them from actual narcotics, the consciousness expanders. As a rule, the authorities show less concern about understanding than about healing and punishing.

The time has come to accuse the accusers, or rather, for they are only cogs in the works, the time has come to ask ourselves if, by condemning universal practices, we show that the protection of our heritage matters to us more than the truth and life itself and that we prefer beliefs that, in the end, satisfy naught but our pride.

Rare are those men who know how to make themselves night and to find certitude in the starry expanse of their interior sky.

The majority joylessly attend to their dark tasks. At every step we encounter sullen faces, eyes colored by venom. There is no doubt that injustice is widespread. Does it explain this constant bitterness and hard crease of the mouth? Is it enough to "transform the world," to "change life"? I think the evil goes deeper. Man has been stricken in his very core, eaten away as if by acid.

---

*[the cosmos of hallucinogenic dreams. —*Ed.*]

It is true that he only becomes aware of this situation fleetingly and, so to speak, obliquely.

His passions, his works, his wars distract him, just like the games that complicate his free time. Everything happens as if he, in order to hide an invincible sorrow, is erecting walls laden with weapons and flowers between that sorrow and himself.

It so happens that Western religion and philosophy both strive to convince us that this sorrow has no discernable cause and is actually invincible. They claim we are unhappy because we are lucid. This, according to religion, is because sin has broken the original covenant and established an essential distance between man and God, but, philosophy adds, this rupture is necessary; the fall is actually an ascension. We have lost our innocence, the empty serenity of animals: so be it. However, by opposing ourselves to the divine law, which is to say, nature, we invented the mind.

It is true we are divided, and this division is an evil, which appears to consciousness as a stain and a sorrow, but this internal fissure is also the sign of the human and, if I may say so, of the very humanity of man. It is, like Jacob's limp, the proof of his being a chosen one.

There is little doubt that healing is the fundamental purpose of all our activity. For religion as for philosophy, it is unification: the victory of good over evil, love over discord, mind over flesh, and, finally, man over nature. It is the Communion of saints and the Universal Republic.

Only—and this is the major point—the West always imagines the unifying process as a slow progression, a fierce struggle. The obstacles are numerous, and we should, as almost all our books teach us, "overcome" and "eliminate" them. This is to say, we cannot obtain salvation, the peace of unity, here and now, on this Earth or in this moment in which we now find ourselves in history. Its place is heaven or the future. Here and now, night surrounds us. This is how the church and revolution speak to us. Only the carmine line sketched by the horizon keeps despair and the demons of the absurd at bay.

Although cursory, these observations explain, I believe, the discomfort that contemplative doctrines inspire in most of the Western religious thinkers and philosophers. The West has formed a dualistic image of man's relationship with the universe. What this means, simply, is that we take our obsessive contradictions for reality and also attribute to work a value that is, strictly speaking, salvific. For us, it is not a question of contemplating but of thinking and doing. Whoever seeks salvation in the present is asserting that the world, here and now, is perfect and that those who deny it have neither eyes to see nor ears to hear. He stands opposed to the entire Western tradition. His language is, undoubtedly, identical to that of the gospels, but, for this very reason, he is irritating and scandalous. He is the quintessential enemy.

The German philosopher Georg Wilhelm Friedrich Hegel and his disciples understood this point perfectly. Hence, the hatred inspired in them specifically by India and generally by all the contemplative doctrines. In their eyes, the silent felicity of the Eastern sage is necessarily illusory. His attitude is a denial of the human condition and is manifested in the realm of action in the form of pure violence, a violence that justifies that of the philosopher. (An illustrious reviewer of the phenomenology goes so far as to declare that if we cannot communicate with the Eastern sage, it is lawful to kill him.)

In other words, from the moment we identify dualistic consciousness with good—a consciousness, it is important to stress, that is also the ordinary guarded consciousness, the colorless light that bathes our gestures and thoughts—we are obliged to identify ecstatic consciousness with evil.

Oneness is thinkable, undoubtedly, but according to Western religious thinkers and philosophers, it is not something that can be experienced. It is "instant," a luminous promise, the oneiric fusion of the absolute and the relative, drunkenness. All that can be built on this sand are smoke castles.

Ecstatic consciousness, which no longer sees the contradictions, is in the lie. Its error is most serious because it denies the value of work, for which it substitutes its futile contemplations. It is passive, inert, and, what's more, arrogant because it believes it is one with the Divinity, whereas it instead allows itself to slide into the neighboring animal condition. It is outside all doing and therefore outside man.

This, in my opinion, is the principal reason for the preventive measures that consciousness expanders spontaneously inspire the public and the press to call for. Christianity—at least official Christianity—is dying; Socrates' mummy crumbles to dust, but we continue to imbibe this dust unknowingly. It is blended with the spirit of the times.

Anyone who uses "hallucinogens" is then a deviant. (The name *hallucinogens* given to them justifies all interventions.) In fact, from the perspective that remains our own, the adept can seek nothing but consolation and refuge.

He asks the imagination to save him from what is, even though the purpose of human effort is to change what is, or to hasten the great coming.

He is sinning against the mind. For, let me repeat, the mind on this Earth is ordinary consciousness. Nothing higher exists, so any escape from it is necessarily headed lower.

Eastern thought attributes an entirely different meaning to human dissatisfaction. Therefore, the Eastern attitude toward consciousness expanders is much less harsh.

For the East, the world and man are both a dream in which the mind has been buried "from the very beginning." We have committed no sin; by seeking to break the enchantment of *maya* (illusion), we are in no way rising up against the divine law.

Anguish is the daughter of illusion, and illusion is precisely the Western dualistic notion. The truth is unity, absolute oneness. Consequently we cannot walk in its direction and attain it. If I may put it this way: Man's place in nature is just like that of the trees and the wind, and nature is just as human as our books and our factories.

What ensues from this, contrary to Hegel's opinion, is that the Eastern sage does not deny the value of doing. He simply does not oppose nature's inertia, and hence does not sanctify it. In his eyes man acts like grass grows, and vice versa.

If anguish is the daughter of illusion, illusion is the daughter of ignorance, that is to say, the poor use we make of our intellect. In fact, we are literally drugged by ignorance. We are consequently hallucinating and incapable of seeing things "as they are" (Sanskrit: *yathâbhûtam*). In order to heal ourselves, it is our right and even our duty to resort to every imaginable subterfuge.

It is the hastening of deliverance that is the purpose of various disciplines, such as exercises of concentration, fasting, and continence, but also certain dangerous or bizarre practices that seem to flout morality and "common sense."

The purpose of all ascetic practices is to inspire an explosion that will pull the mind out of its cosmic slumber.

From this perspective, which as we see is totally different from the Western one, it is not possible to consider a priori the man who uses consciousness expanders as a criminal, on the condition, of course, that awakening is the purpose of his research.

Undoubtedly, the expanders are ambivalent and double-edged weapons, but much the same can be said about traditional practices. There are many inns on the path of the paternal house, and each sports the signboard of eternity.

Having said this, it is obviously not enough to state that sacramental plants can indicate the way, the "door without a door" of awakening, nor, as I have done here, to abstractly challenge old prejudices, an attitude that is basically provincial.

My preferences are quite clear, but it is now time to justify them and, in order to do so, to explain as clearly as possible the actions and effects of consciousness expanders. This is the primary purpose of this book.

When someone takes a consciousness expander, the action of the plant or powder first manifests in the form of a radical and forlorn sense of solitude comparable to that of the person on his deathbed.

We suddenly discover there is nothing that others can do for us and that we are naked, surrounded and inhabited by countless perils, that "everything is an abyss. . . ."

Only an invincible love of life, an adamantine certitude—let's say the word: a *faith*—can help us during these vertiginous moments to withstand the assaults of despair.

It so happens that modern reason is unaware of the difference between learning and knowledge, showing an inscrutable and serene face, a divine equanimity to human weakness. This point cannot be stressed too emphatically. Taking modern reason at its word, the only things that truly exist and deserve our attention are the community, the movement of history, and cosmic laws. Beneath "objective" and "scientific" appearances, it is abstract. To fingers seeking a grip, it offers a hard, smooth, slippery, and cold surface.

A thousand shifting veils in everyday life conceal this evidence from us.

We do not distinguish the truly strong ideas, those with the power to sustain the mind in the midst of ordeals, from those that possess only the appearance of strength provided by the fallacious authority conferred on them by widespread diffusion. We forget that we are not pure intellect and that abstractions can hold no value for an individual who is suffering and scared.

We only remember this truth when we are physically stricken. However, it is too late; the gulf has already opened beneath our feet, and we descend into the darkness bearing a dead lantern and a glass sword.

It is the explosion of this black revelation reflected by faces convulsing in anxiety that the newsweeklies, with feigned indignation, have been displaying for some time.* The public is given the impression that these photographs illustrate the "ravages of drugs." In fact, we are dealing with something entirely different here: a realization.

No spiritual food worthy of the name has ever been suggested to these young people. On the contrary, doctrines have been imposed

---

*This book was originally written in 1967 and refers here to articles published by particular newspapers at the time (editor's note, 1994 edition).

on them, with the accent of authority, that present an image of life, love, the universe, and the Divinity that could legitimately be labeled as homicide.

It would undoubtedly be dangerous to claim that LSD is harmless: no substance that turns the mind upside down this drastically could be. However, one thing is certain: the majority of the tragedies that can occur under its influence cannot be attributed to this substance. The true causes of these tragedies are the ideas that have been inculcated into these investigators since childhood, all these "Hasnamussian"* ideas, as the Russian spiritual teacher and author G. I. Gurdjieff humorously called them, that is to say, the life-devouring and toxic ideas that the investigators have incorporated long before taking LSD, without ever doubting the poisoning to which they were victims.

If the man who takes a consciousness expander claims as his own the "fiduciary values," as the French poet, essayist, and philosopher Paul Valéry called them, the collapse of these values will necessarily bring about that of his own. LSD destroys his beliefs and thereby destroys him at the same time, for in these extreme moments, he becomes one with what he believes. It is impossible to treat this like a game, as we all, more or less, unfortunately, try to do. Therefore, the tragedies that the press accuses LSD of causing are not due to this substance.

By shattering the relationship that consciousness maintains with the world, LSD reveals to us something most people only discover on their deathbeds, the fact that the majority of our ideas are only, as someone has rightly put it, ideas. It compels us to become aware of our inhumanity and the atrocious implications. In this sense, LSD is certainly dangerous.

---

*[psychopathic. —*Ed.*]

But I must add that it is only dangerous for those who confuse learning with knowledge and seek elsewhere what can be found here, giving in to the centrifugal movement of the intellect, worshipping the god of books and imagining that "objective" and "scientific" truths can replace bread and wine.

❊

In ordinary life, the strange is always localized. You can always point at it with your finger and say it is here or there.

On the other hand, for the person who has taken a consciousness expander, the strange is everywhere. Sensations, emotions, and thoughts all have a slightly indescribable difference. You see more, you understand more, but most importantly, you see and understand differently. Rather than the object, it is the way you look at things that undergoes a transformation.

It is obviously extremely difficult to express a change of this nature. I can describe a unicorn, but how do I describe the world from the unicorn's point of view? The documents we currently possess allow no answer to this question.

Among the many investigators, there are obviously quite a number—the majority, I suppose—who have given little thought to the difference that exists between speaking and writing and to the fact that words are a collective property and do not belong to the individual, that the "the flower absent from every bouquet" is the flower I see and there is nothing so difficult as showing it to others.

What does a man feel when he is in love? What does a woman feel? Words cause divergences to appear, which may be merely verbal. We can at least imagine that love is made by a new entity: the couple, an archangel into which the partners momentarily dissolve. If this is the truth of the act, it is absurd to believe that the man is "active" and the woman "passive," yet this is the postulate no one dreams of challenging.

This is how language is twice a traitor: first it makes us believe that because our interlocutor gives objects the same names as we do, we understand him; second, when we become aware of how difficult the exchange is our consciousness makes us believe that the obstacle is insurmountable and that all understanding is necessarily fragmentary and illusory.

With the exception of the Belgian poet, writer, and painter Henri Michaux, I know of no one who has tried to make others see or feel. (Solier observes the discipline of the arcane with infinite circumspection. He only describes the approaches and the sanctuary.)

Generally, the investigators just let the words spill out to a certain extent. They innocently respond to questions, and those listening to them and noting down their observations share the same attitude. No one remarks on the fact that would strike anyone reading these notes with a cool head: the vast majority of these narratives offer no real information on the "profane." The absolute strangeness of the experience is simply described; it is not expressed.

For example, we are told that under the influence of LSD, a person sees "colors." So be it, but do we not see colors in ordinary life as well? What makes them different? This question seems to interest no one.

There is no doubt that this difference could be indescribable.

However, this is precisely the point to which I wish to draw attention: nobody is asking those who talk about the consciousness expanders to do the work required of any writer.

Yet it is evident that before passing judgment on LSD or peyote, it is absolutely necessary to form as precise an image as possible of what happens when it is consumed, and it is not possible to obtain this image from individuals, no matter how intelligent they may be, who have a naive belief in the transparency of words.

What happens when we read a document concerning sacramental plants? We do not read it as we would a poem or a novella. Indeed, we know that the author has taken a "drug," and this piece of information changes our perspective, unbeknownst to us.

It is less what is said than what is left unsaid that excites our curiosity and fascinates us. Without perceiving that we are doing so, we add to what we are reading a quality that is, objectively speaking, absent. We superimpose on an often disappointing and flat text a kind of opalescent vibration formed by the image we have of the "drug." This engenders a great many misunderstandings.

However, there is also another cause for these misunderstandings. It is my feeling that scholars and journalists have committed a grave error. They have placed all the testimonies on the same level, as if all were of equal value. In truth, they have shown a preference for those narratives that display a spontaneous, crazed, and scattered nature.

Does it go without saying that the tape recording provides a more "authentic" image than the text?

Even worse is the fact that they have lent their ears to the phrases but have not taken into account the silences, which are sometimes long and painful and—above all—much more meaningful than the phrases, inasmuch as these silences are telling of the mind's dismay when it has great difficulty finding expression.

In short, scholars and journalists (there are exceptions, of course) have posited—without truly understanding, it seems, the implications of their attitude—that if, under the influence of mind-expanding substances, we express ourselves in a confused language, it is because these substances plunge us into confusion.

No one is asked to provide a precise description of his impressions during an earthquake. However, it appears quite natural to cast doubt on the mental stability of the investigator of consciousness expanders who is incapable, while "being quaked," of expressing himself as he normally would.

What we are dealing with here is a conviction that is hard to justify, to say the least. This is a conviction that is entirely Western to boot and one that gives shape to all our philosophies.

Accustomed since Plato (I am also thinking of the beginning of the Gospel of John) to regard the word as the immediate reflection of the mind, we also view the clear word as the reflection of a clear mind. From something that seems so patently obvious to us we inevitably draw the following conclusion: anyone who talks like a madman is a madman.

Of course, I am not at all certain of being able to express the unicorn's point of view. It is already almost impossible to speak about daily life. Practically all authors exaggerate, simplify, dramatize, and omit, in short, turn the situation to their best possible advantage. If André Breton is cited, someone who was so wonderfully attuned to the sinuous nature of the incident, it can be seen that authors generally confuse the likely with the true. Like mercury, what spills between the fingers divides into thousands of tenacious globules.

Nevertheless, we can attempt to circumscribe the inexpressible, to make others feel what resists being put into words, to explain, when all is said and done, why the unicorn's point of view escapes speech.

1

THE TURNING FANFARE

Dark strangers, if we began!

"MEMORY," ARTHUR RIMBAUD

In 1956 one of my oldest friends came to France. He came like the king of Salem, Melchizedek, bearing bread and wine. However, this bread and wine gave every indication of being poison.

It was a greenish powder with large seeds that smelled like mildew and had a very bitter taste. The plant, which David had dried and ground to make this powder, was regarded by the American Indians of Arizona as sacred, and they called it "Christ's gift to the red man." They would consume it on Saturday evenings and spend the night in front of a fire; the following morning, they would attend the religious services at the neighboring church. To the pastor's protests, they responded that the white man had railroads and airplanes, but they had this plant, this cactus. One was compensation for the other.

This peyote cactus was completely harmless, according to David.

He had me read English author Aldous Huxley's study and various scientific publications that he had brought with him. I was intrigued but hostile. My hostility would have been much sharper had I read Michaux's *Miserable Miracle*, which had just been published, but I would only get wind of that book later.

A rift formed in our friendship. David refused to take my moral and intellectual objections seriously. In his opinion it was fear and fear alone beneath my refusal to cross the threshold of the unknown. Whether intentional or not, a slight air of scorn began to color his affection.

And I felt the exact same sentiment toward him. Whether peyote was harmless or not, whether or not it was addictive, its use implied a denial of reality. Worse, it was a cowardly refusal disguised as an escape to adventure.

The prospect of seeing and feeling what a powder forced me to see and feel, to even temporarily renounce my freedom, filled me with horror. I had no desire to dream; I wanted to live. David smiled and shook his head: "That's not it at all. . . . You cannot understand."

However, during that summer, dark forces were storming in and carrying me away on their wave of mud.

I ran out of arguments to oppose David's. The use of hallucinogens was a weakness: so be it. One proof among others, it implied a cowardly refusal: again, so be it. I needed to increase the distance between my failures and myself. If the sole available refuge was an oneiric miracle, I would consent to hide there.

I no longer knew how to live, believe, and love. I was already a lost man, might as well consume my perdition. It was the first of August 1956 that I attempted this version of suicide.

Irritable and anxious, I paced the hundred steps of the garden of the house I was occupying that summer in Antibes. I detested myself; I detested what I saw, what I felt, and what I was doing. I then headed down Ermitage Road. I felt a moment of distraction. It lasted for (a second?) the time it took to raise my eyes to a laurel hedge. I was in paradise.

I had to take peyote numerous times before realizing the importance of the moment of distraction. It is the passage into the unknown, a gift of the self, a gift without which it is impossible to cross the threshold. On the first day, I simply noted that fear and doubt had vanished, that I could no longer grasp how anyone could fear and doubt. This was paradise. A world in which the "big questions," the questions all humans ask, were emptied of their content. A world *full of meaning*.

I had spent thirty years sleeping. Now I was shaking off the glamour of the night; I got up. Phantoms, morbid imaginings, "the transparencies and thickenings of the dream," as Victor Hugo said, all that was wild and nebulous had dissipated. I was finally free, truly free; I was the master of my body and my mind; I no longer feared death.

Before taking peyote, I thought that this plant, like others of similar nature, created an unreality. No matter how interesting and enthusing the studies of the French poet Charles Baudelaire and the English essayist Thomas De Quincy were, they mainly contained descriptions of dreams or distorted iridescent spaces made up of echoes and reflections, of spaces that a momentary disruption of the senses seemed to relieve of their density.

It so happens that far from veiling reality, peyote unveils it, and, because the sensation that accompanies this unveiling is glorious, it can legitimately be called a revelation. Peyote revealed to me a world that was finally real, and real because it was full of meaning, engorged with meaning like a fruit is with flavor. It removed the film of insignificance that ordinarily covers things. It showed them to me in their nakedness. Appearance no longer concealed essence, but expressed it. Rather, the distinction I made between essence and appearance had vanished. The tree was completely a tree, the stone was a stone, and the sky was sky. And me, I was me.

There is a barbaric word in bureaucratic parlance, *normalization,* that is especially familiar to outsiders, people like me caught in a situation that is desperately and even ontologically irregular. This word precisely describes the sensation caused by peyote when you surrender and give yourself to it. Peyote normalizes. Each time I have been able to abandon myself to it, I have experienced the joy of no longer being beneath all the stars of the sky an exception, a crippled person, one of those beings who is neither an angel nor an animal and who "in seeking to become an angel turns into a beast." Simply, a man.

I knew exactly on which branch in which olive tree this cicada was singing, under which leaf that cricket was hiding, around which rose this bee was buzzing. The breeze playing in the telephone lines caused the reeds rising out of the windbreaks to sway with a soft growl. People went in and out of the neighboring villa, opening and closing doors, talking. Cars were twisting down the cape road.

All of these different sounds, far from producing a confused effect, wove clearly defined relationships with each other, as if they were producing a musical composition. Each was necessary, each was born in a particular point of space and at a particular moment in time, and their disappearance created a crystalline void, out of which a new vibration would immediately arise. All together, they were like a fugue with neither end nor origin, and which, nonetheless, did not deny time, for each of its figures had the perfection of a finished object and the budding density of a promise.

This fugue was a sonorous expression of divine nature, of active reason. A permanent miracle was the very law of the cosmos.

How could I doubt this miracle and this law, given that I experienced them? If I had the adequate knowledge, I would have transcribed the architecture of this "rural concert" into the language of music.

I felt as if I were seeing shapes and colors for the first time. In ordinary life, I know rather than see that things have three dimensions. They are tools or obstacles. I perceive them through the goal on which I have set my sights. At that moment, I was not aiming at any goal, and I could see the purity of things. Stretching out my hand, I felt the heat of the day slide like silk through my fingers. Space was massive and palpitating. It was like invisible flesh unfolding under my gaze.

However, I did not see the colors that Huxley mentioned. Of course, the blue of the sky could be compared to a sapphire and the green of the grass to an emerald, but only to indicate, through the very poverty of the comparison, the impotence of descriptive language. In fact, the green of the grass did not exactly resemble that of an emerald. It was an absolutely unique green, the green of this grass, of that tuft sprouting at the edge of the path, and it was comparable to nothing else, not even the green of a neighboring tuft of grass.

It was in this sense that this green was precious, like a precious stone, like an emerald. It was rare, infinitely rare, and therefore infinitely precious. It was peerless and, consequently, more precious than the most beautiful emerald, but as soon as the thought was formed, I once again ran up against the ambiguity of words.

For what I said about the grass can surely be applied to the emerald, to each and every emerald.

This was in no way destructive of the dignity of language, the sovereign mystery; I could name and did name this absolutely unique form: "grass" and this name was accurate. However, I could and did give the same name to the neighboring tuft of grass, and I could say this admirable thing about both the grass and the emerald: both were green.

I was standing differently. I knew how to hold myself up. I possessed the mastery of an animal or a savage. Here's a strange thing: I could walk barefoot. My foot adapted to the uneven surface of the ground perfectly and distributed the weight of my body over the pebbles and gravel in such a way that had there been pieces of broken glass or live coals, I would have effortlessly walked over them.

I was more agile, quicker, stronger, and had greater flexibility, and this increase in my physical abilities was easily verifiable. The tennis ball flew to its target as if a champion were handling the racket.

I was open and simple. I no longer feared suffering or the judgment of others: suffering because it was incapable of breaking the inner diamond, the judgment of others because it did not target my singularity but only the inevitably imperfect manifestation of the universal man. The universal man was an abstraction, a verbal idol.

I perceived an enormous number of things that normally escaped my attention, and from this extension of my faculties, the vision of divine nature was born.

In fact, I could clearly see the reason why this oak, for example, had a particular form rather than another. The gnarled surface of the trunk brought out, exactly as if in a painting, the granular texture of the neighboring wall; the tree's roots were twisted and hunched because the grass sprouting between their forks was smooth and flexible.

In other words, I noted that the universe was a piece of work, essentially identical to the works of men and subject to the same laws: a composed, conceived, meditated, organized piece of work whose every detail had its own place in the whole. Chance was an invention of laziness, an appearance that would dissipate beneath a more attentive gaze.

However, the difference persisted. It was immense. Human artists were imitators and simplifiers. They offered an image of divine nature, but this image was always and inevitably partial, superficial, and crude. Moreover, it was static. Divine nature, on the other hand, was alive. It was continually changing. It was "becoming," yet—and this was the surprising thing—each moment of this becoming was perfect. It did not travel through the dissolution that intelligence uses to distinguish each moment from the following one.

The truth, the inexplicable but indubitable truth, was that infinite invention was one side of the principle whose other side was eternal law. Absolute freedom was the same thing as its apparent opposite, absolute necessity, and as I say this, I am perpetuating the dualist illusion despite myself. It is necessary to go boldly beyond logic and state that in divine nature, freedom is necessity and necessity is freedom. They are only divided when seen through the prism of reason. If someone cannot resist the imperative necessity of giving a name to what I am talking about, he should restrict himself to the vocabulary of "magic" and name it, for example, the Effluvium.

My joy was mixed with dizziness. The contrast that appeared between human genius and what I could only call divine genius was too violent. In a certain sense, I understood this genius because, as I said, its work was essentially identical to that which I was familiar with. However, the difference that stood between the work of the divine and the work of men was only all the more confusing.

The intention that animated the divine order embraced the vast efflorescence of individual intentions. It spontaneously wed the boldest, the most bizarre, and the craziest innovations. It was a dancer who no change of rhythm could surprise or cause to flinch. It was inhuman because it was superhuman; although all the movements, which indicated the consciousness emanating from it, were intelligible.

I was able to understand either this or that. I could imagine an individual for whom this question would not arise at all and who had the ability to grasp this and that simultaneously. However, I was unable to even conceive of a human being capable of becoming one with the unfathomable multitude of all beings, from the grain of sand to the sun, from the protoplasm to the human being, because such a being outstripped common measure.

The world was—and beyond any shadow of a doubt—"the living, the vastness in full bloom."* The very simplicity of it stupefied me. It was nothing "other" than myself. It was only bigger, but never mind if I am overusing this word; it was infinitely bigger. It extended beyond all boundaries and in every direction.

---

*This expression was used by Victor Hugo. As I will often use the word *God* in this book, it is important for me to underline that my understanding of this word is totally different from the meaning accorded to it by Christianity, a religion that I would willingly refer to as Paulinism, or even Satanism, because this religion worships he whom its so-called founder calls "the father of lies."

Personally, I consider Jesus either as an avatar of Krishna, like the Asians do, or as a bodhisattva, if you prefer Buddhist terminology.

In fact, my religion is Victor Hugo's religion, exactly the one that Anglo-French scholar, writer, and broadcaster Denis Saurat described a long time ago in a memorable book. Naturally, because my God is Victor Hugo's God, my attitude toward "Christianity" is necessarily identical (or almost) to his.

My ever-keener awareness of a tremendous disparity became agonizing. I recalled the biblical warning of the fatally dazzling awe that threatens the seer. I sometimes felt that if I lost control of my indwelling strength, this awe could transport me before the throne and thrust on me a vision of intolerable glory.

I perceived the perfect similarity between freedom and necessity because I retained this sense of harmony. This primarily meant that I remained aware of the relationship that every sensation, every object established with all the others, in other words, the place that each one occupied in the structure that language expresses.

As soon as I forgot this—which happened several times—a potential darkness surfaced.

Walking through the shadow that a tree cast over the path, I suddenly began to shiver. The sun was shining; the weather was glorious, yet my teeth were chattering. Why? For a fraction of a second I thought I was sick, or crazy. Fortunately, surprised by the sensation, I realized that I had given it my total attention and that I had isolated this sensation from the others and therefore, if I may put it this way, made it an absolute. It was not the sensation that had produced this glacial impression but the sudden involuntary concentration of my mind.

It was also necessary to remain attentive to the harmony in order to avoid hallucinating. If I became absorbed in the contemplation of a bark or a wall, faces would appear, clusters of hilarious and phosphorescent faces, a hateful effervescence of heads.

The contemplated object lost its identity and its name. It was no longer one object among others; it became the Object. The entire universe was condensed in it, in a diabolical form.

I felt no fatigue, but I sensed that the strength I was enjoying did not belong to me. It was exactly as if—painlessly, of course—a forceps had forced a passage through my ordinarily joined flesh, which my everyday consciousness used to communicate with a much vaster consciousness. The action of the peyote seemed to consist essentially in the maintaining of this opening.

It was also as if I had miraculously acquired the mastery of a juggler or tightrope walker. Losing balance and falling was always an imminent possibility, but I played with this imminence, with the void opening beneath my feet. I used it to move the swaying and vibrations of the rope on which I was walking.

In the trees, the sky, the rocks, and everywhere, I could see the movement of the vital power that I had named the Effluvium.

Fire flowed, the sky flowed, the trees and the rocks flowed. Only they had different "rhythms." I told David, "If we were always in this state . . ." He finished my thought: ". . . we would be mad."

I had the right to see, but on the condition that I remembered that I was an ordinary man, and not even that, alas, but a weak and troubled man with no backbone. Also, I had to draw from the memory of the Effluvium the courage to do so without the plant that had procured me this vision.*

In fact, as I said earlier, I had not set my sights on any goal. Under the influence of peyote, I could aim at nothing. I could neither make any plans nor finish any undertakings I had already commenced. I was completely passive. To have the right to sojourn

---

*This is an important point. Peyote is a *master* in the Eastern sense of the word. Thanks to it, we can know the goal of initiation, but in order to attain it, we must become athletes of the mind, and for this, one must strive long and hard. As long as we are not permanently in the state induced by the use of peyote, we are nothing ("absolute shit," as Gurdjieff would have said). Just like the time-honored master, peyote teaches us to do without. To those who ask that the work be done in their place, peyote inflicts thirty strokes of the stick.

in paradise, I had to become "like God"; I had to unite, as he did, invention and law, necessity and freedom. It did not suffice to be a passive participant in the divine order. I had to learn how to become an active participant as well, to transcend any opposition that persisted, even in my state of bliss, inasmuch as I could distinguish my current state from my ordinary state and, therefore, put them into opposition.

It was the "telescopic vision" that gave me my greatest palpable joys. It was enough for me to stare at any one part of the sky in order to pierce the gaseous envelope of the Earth and see the stars in the deep night of space. As for this envelope itself, I could discern its movements and stratifications with perfect clarity. Gusts of wind, like diaphanous rivers, rolled over one another. Sometimes a current spilled out and bouquets of volutes edged in frost and prismatic blossoms would form.

From a horizontal perspective, the clouds appeared to rest on their shadows as if on a blue pillar. From a vertical perspective, their internal structure became clearer.

I am speaking here about the light clouds that the summer breezes form and break apart into what usually look like pale, tattered wisps.

Peyote makes this nebulous mass translucent; it becomes an intricate mass of ramified and mobile volumes: supple, milky, and living volumes that are as fragile as glass. These volumes are linked to one another by denser knots of vapor. Slightly curved innervations separate from these knots and form new knots, which in turn break up into even frailer threads, similar to long phalanxes.

I admit it was difficult to refuse a consciousness to these large beings. They seemed to be ceding to the space surrounding them, ecstatically and languorously. Their march was a perpetual dawn.

The breeze running through them gave rise to a whiteness that immediately swelled, expanded, and dissolved. They condensed, only to give themselves away.

I wanted to mix with the human crowd, to enter the glorious multitude. To do this, walking down to the beach would suffice.

Unfortunately, I had a distressing encounter with a crippled person on my way there.

At first, I could see naught but a painful interlocking of jerky movements. Then basic features emerged: short pants from which emerged a pair of legs the color of watered milk and large, hobnailed shoes that hit the ground alternately, like hammers.

The unfortunate soul appeared to be oddly *proud* of his handicap. Yes, this is how I am, he seemed to be saying, and if you don't like it, you can just go some other damn place.

When I walked past him, he cast me a glare full of hatred. This was understandable. I was at the peak of my strength, health, and youth, while he . . . However, what bothered me most was my inability to help him. Nobody could. He was sick; that was obvious, but he refused to admit it. On the contrary, he considered his illness to be original; it was his pride and joy.

While I was having these painful thoughts, three women appeared. I started involuntarily. They too were crippled, all three of them.

Their appearance was different from that of the man, slower and weaker. His zigzag gait was replaced by their waddle, but they were no less rickety than he was.

A clinic specializing in diseases affecting the joints must have been located somewhere in the neighborhood, and this man and these women were undoubtedly residents there.

I saw short, pleated skirts, cork-soled sandals, shirts open to the bra straps, dark glasses with rhinestone-studded frames, patches of reddened skin, fuzzy hair, and jockey helmets with visors stretching into coal shovels.

The faces of all three were contorted by the same grimace, as if they were sucking on an intolerably sour lemon.

I had to reach the beach in order to understand the truth, the terrible truth. They were all crippled people, and those who possessed beautiful bodies were the worst. Glued to the tops of pillars of grace and strength were heads that were batrachian in their stupidity or simian-like in their brutality.

All of them, the beautiful and the ugly, the young and old, had the exaggerated characters of allegories. Beneath this parasol, Laziness was lounging. Kneeling at its side was Avarice. Elsewhere, Vanity was grooming itself beneath the gaze of Lust.

Terrified, I turned my attention to the sea. The curve of the globe delicately arched its surface. Here, the sandy bottom, over which the sun was playing, gilded its vitreous density; further on, it took on a viridescent hue, a vaporous tint of jade; further still, it turned violet. Silvery ripples ran over it. The shadows of the waves filled the transparency of its sinuous, dancing lines, which would suddenly split up, caught in the meshes of scintillation. Above the horizon, the clouds were ecstatically separating their crystalline offshoots.

Turning my gaze to the beach once again, I saw that almost all the children were beautiful and fresh. They were playing, quarreling, going about their business. I found this comforting. Later, I would sometimes happen to cross paths with a normal individual among the adults: a tramp, for example, by the side of the road. He was cooking some kind of stew, he was happy, he was simple, he flowed, and he allowed the Effluvium to flow. No doubt his nose was swollen and red, and his eyelids heavy. He was filthy, tattered, and grubby, but the essential was intact.

Then a woman passed by, a completely ordinary woman— simple, serious, placid, attentive to the things that mattered: home, children, and savoring life.

She was ordinary, as ordinary as the others were baroque. This was the confusing thing, this disruption of proportions, this inexplicable and numerical supremacy of madness. The vast majority of human beings wore false noses, like carnival characters. They were coated with greasy paint, sporting comical wigs, posing twisted and motionless. You could wonder how they held these poses and, more important, how they tolerated these useless vices, suffocating beliefs, and abstract sentiments, day and night. In fact, they seemed to be in terrible suffering, yet, not one of them thought of removing his hideous costume and bathing.

However, this woman and this tramp and some others whom I saw later participated in the harmony with perfect submissiveness and grace. Their faces were bare. They were not pretending to live; they were alive.

Thus, from the very first experience, I was introduced to evil. As all the masters taught us, God was everywhere. However, most men worshipped an empty form, the idol that the greatest Western master had named the lie and the father of the lie. This false god, this idol, was society. Not that society was itself evil. Like the rest, it belonged to the divine order. The evil came from the fact that its demands had been established in absolute terms and deified, so that the genuine absolute, the true God, was veiled by the false.

Why? I found no answer to this question. Thus, from my first contact with peyote, I was certain of one thing and doubted another.

In my heart of hearts, I did not doubt that I had seen things as they were, in their truth, but my intelligence was balked. God was everywhere, and he was absent to these men and women who denied him.

They were not part of the divine order, which was nevertheless all embracing. So, the unlimited had a limit. This contradiction seemed insolvable and, whether I liked it or not, forced me to doubt that which I did not doubt: the fact that the euphoric state, which I had wandered in for a day, was reality.

This was the first of my "grand days." The following ones were alike and different. It was the *real life* that Rimbaud spoke of, although his predilection for the unusual led him to dark and dangerous places.

The following day, one thing became immediately certain: I no longer asked the infinitely painful question that had been torment-ing me since my adolescence.

I thought I had taken a "drug," a poisonous and, if I may put it this way, Baudelairean substance that, for a few hours, allowed me to imagine that success was rushing in on golden wings, that all my desires were fulfilled, all my wishes granted.

I had consciously sought illusion, false salvation, false energy, and false happiness in the terrible hope of consuming my perdition.

I had expected to see diaphanous palaces, fairies, a nocturnal Orient of platinum opulence. I had also hoped to acquire a taste for these visions (even though David had insisted on several occasions that peyote did not give this taste), to become one of those unfortunate souls who, in order to obtain a little powder, is willing to steal, even kill.

What I desired was to roll right down to the bottom of the slope, so that there was no longer the question of winning, or even strug-gling, to attain stagnation and stupefaction, to wind up in an asylum.

Terrified of responsibilities, I had already felt a similar temptation toward the end of my adolescent years, the black desire of folly. Be a man? Why? It signified wanting, doing, working... "I will never work!" I wanted to become the weakest of the weak, the one who nobody asks anything of, the spectral laughter evoked by the word *junkie*.

Yet, peyote had given me quite the opposite; it had given me a new and *permanent* strength; it had made me a man who was stronger, more mature, and lucid. This was noticeable from the very next day. I was changed, and changed for the better; my perception had undergone a change, but more important, peyote had brought a liberating answer to the question I mentioned earlier.

I was a *visionary,* in the sense that Swedish philosopher and scientist Emanuel Swedenborg or English poet Robert Blake could give to this word. Not that I lived, like they did, in intimate acquaintance with "spirits" or that it was enough for me to turn my gaze toward the sky and see "white nations in joy," as Rimbaud would.

However, the fact remains that I was separated from the voices and the apparitions by a fog thinner than in the case of most men.

Unfortunately, since the scientific revolution, it has become difficult—and in truth, almost impossible—to consider the visionary gift as a privilege. Even the insane possess this gift. Is there really any difference between what I call a vision and what science calls a hallucination? This question had darkened my entire youth.

For a long time, I had forced myself to opt for reason, to break the emotional tie linking me to imaginings that had virtually covered my window of lucidity with a fantastical frost.

However, the reasonable option was also the option of despair.

If the scientific explanation was true in my case, the only honest attitude toward the universe and the human condition was the nihilistic one. With science, the livid apostolate of violence and suicide <u>triumphed</u>. What is the point of widening the horizons of our knowledge? We know what is essential: that we are sparks that have appeared by chance on the surface of the abyss and that we are doomed to extinction.

Paradoxically, reason (or at least what I called reason) was spurring me into a state of madness far worse than the one into which this acceptance of wonders was dragging me.

Peyote threw the sword of Brennos into the debate.

I am not trying to say that I had absolute certainties during the first few grand days, as I called them, or since. I was not in the least exempted from believing. In order to affirm the authenticity of my visions, I still had to step into the void.

However, from then on, I could do it without trembling.

Peyote had changed the conditions under which the act of faith is fulfilled.

I could, in all conscience, deny the scientific explanation in my case. In other words, I could posit that even though there is no doubt that hallucinatory phenomena exist, there are also some phenomena that can lawfully be described as visionary and that distinguish themselves from the former by a specific set of traits. Sometimes, an individual can leave the common realm without getting lost in the gray moors of insanity, but, in order to understand this, it is necessary to study the effects of peyote.

Peyote essentially dilates all faculties—all except the intellect, I think. In other words, *peyote shows you nothing at all: it temporarily removes a barrier that ordinarily prevents seeing.**

---

*Observations seem to show that LSD, a substance that I am not familiar with, but which, apparently, produces effects that are similar or identical to those of peyote, acts by inhibiting the activity of the brain to a certain extent.

If these observations are correct, strangely enough, they bring a scientific caution to the ancient eastern Indian doctrine, which has always maintained that the *rising* of consciousness can only be obtained by the *diminishing* of cerebral activity. Having said this, it is important to add that one must be wary always of observations made during experiments held under scientific supervision, which is, save certain exceptions, the worst condition possible. After all, the bird of Minerva is an owl. The mouse can hardly behave in a natural way under its cold eye.

It is important to stress here that I am now describing the main effect of peyote. Under its influence, one can conjure up imaginary shows or play with the luminous dust orbiting the mind or dream. There are many investigators who have only sought—and have only found—these empty pleasures, thus coming to the conclusion that peyote is just another narcotic among many others. In my opinion, they are making a mistake; they are making petty use of the cactus, and, to tell the truth, they are wasting their time.

If peyote does in fact—temporarily—erase the fog that ordinarily outlines the scope of attention, then the name by which scholars designate this substance, and other similar substances, is clearly not suitable.

Being nearsighted, I wear glasses. Even the extravagance of the world imposing itself on my gaze as soon as I put them on would not prompt me to qualify what I see through my glasses as "hallucinatory." It is obvious that I do not see things the way they are—yathâbhûtam—nevertheless, I certainly see them more clearly than with the naked eye.

It is true that, if peyote is essentially a stimulant or, more precisely, an awakener, as I believe it to be, it must have an effect on the imagination, as it does on the other faculties. In fact, under its influence, one sees images much more clearly than one ordinarily does—sometimes, so clearly that the difference between the images and physical objects tends to disappear.

Then, hallucinatory superimpositions, in the strict sense of the word, may occur: for example, we may think that the wall is looking at us or that the leaves are talking to us.

The bad news is that most scholars seem to think that the ability to create such illusions constitutes the main characteristic of peyote. They believe this blindly, and this only too well justifies the suspicions of serious investigators and their irritation when it comes to the confidence of many so-called experts describing sacramental plants.

What happened on the day of my initiation? It was as if the limits, which the weakness of my senses ordinarily imposes on their activity, were slowly and dizzyingly dissolving.

One could say that the walls—they were countless—that were stifling me (and worse still, I was unaware of this) were losing their opacity, were becoming transparent and evaporating.

I have already described what I call "telescopic vision," but the powers of my other faculties had increased tremendously as well. Peyote had virtually grafted an extremely powerful amplifier on each of my senses.

I stress these facts because even though some investigators have pointed them out, none of them, to my knowledge, have measured the consequences. Now, it seems to me that these consequences are likely to shatter all our beliefs.

As a matter of fact, before August 1, 1956, I had never dreamt of doubting *the authority of common perception.*

It seemed natural that I should name things: the world, an ensemble of things that all men perceive or can perceive, thanks to the instruments that science places at their disposal.

This dull, drab, and dreary world did not satisfy me, but, since other human beings did not question this either, this came as no surprise to me, nor did I ask myself, thereafter, if universal dissatisfaction came from any kind of perceptional disorder.

I wanted to "change life": it seemed neither possible nor necessary to change my *outlook* on life.

Thus, I confused common perception with normal perception; I must admit that I was not fully aware of the significance of my attitude. Regarding common perception as normal necessarily meant that I should consider as real only those objects that were likewise considered real by all human beings, in other words, only those objects that all human beings had the capacity to perceive.

As a result, I would also regard as suspicious and cast away any perception that noticeably differed from common perception.

Any perception was, in fact, *abnormal* by definition, and this adjective always had a pejorative overtone. Only too often, I happened, as Blake wrote:

> *To see a world in a grain of sand,*
> *And a heaven in a wild flower,*
> *Hold infinity in the palm of your hand,*
> *And eternity in an hour.*

But I stored these moments away (although they alone made existence worthwhile) in the category of unhealthy elation. Under these conditions, I could not give a satisfactory answer to the question that had been tormenting me. Maybe a vision differed from a hallucination, but both were abnormal. In other words, both were bizarre, morbid, equivocal, and, to sum up, repugnant.

Peyote shattered these seeming certainties. It showed me that common perception and normal perception are two completely different things, and we confuse them only because we have an incorrect idea of our sensory abilities.

These abilities are infinitely more extensive than we can imagine. That being said, for reasons I cannot explain, *we generally receive only a third or a quarter of the messages that our organs are capable of transmitting to us.*

This fact, which I yet again cannot explain, is the reason why we regard common perception as normal and also the reason why we regard as real the world in which our monotonous and sparse daily life slips by.

On the day of my initiation, I discovered a world that was different from the one I knew, just as a living woman is different from her portrait.

Nevertheless, the abilities that I possessed—it is impossible to stress this point enough—were perfectly *natural,* inscribed in the structure of my organism. Legs are meant for running as well as walking. The reasons for which I had so far been deprived of these abilities in everyday life eluded all discernment. Yet, here was the astounding thing: in order to enjoy the profound forces of my being, if only for a few hours and on the sly, I had to take a chemical substance.

Common perception is abnormal: this is the fundamental fact. We realize that a strange and tragic handicap is the reason why the world seems gray, dull, and insipid, and that we seek refuge in the imagination and entertainment and temporary oblivion in books and alcohol.

We touch things with felt gloves and look at them through tinted lenses; our ears and noses are blocked up in such a way that we hardly perceive sounds and scents; as for taste, we are only capable of appreciating the strongest ones. In short, it is as if an evil spirit has injected us with a powerful and perfidious anaesthetic.

Since I was enjoying powers that were natural under the influence of peyote, it was obvious that some men who did not need to use this substance necessarily existed (umpteen indications suggest that Gurdjieff was one such man), men who, either from birth or as a result of their efforts, had permanently dispersed that fog that envelops my mind as soon as the effects of peyote weaken, men who were, in comparison with me and the majority, truly normal beings, possessing not just a fraction, but the totality of the abilities that nature had endowed them with.

However, at that moment, this affected me less than the observation that follows: if, henceforth, I considered as abnormal the state that the vast majority considers as normal, and if I considered as unreal the world as it appears to the vigilant or those with ordinary consciousness, I could certainly not, being aware of this, give any credit whatsoever to the judgments made by their consciousnesses.

Any kind of science or philosophy elaborated in a dream state or while intoxicated clearly has very little value. From then on, I denied men in their ordinary state the right to ask certain questions. In truth, they could only provide abstract, fallacious, and arbitrary answers. They were trying to understand the rules of a game that was missing crucial pieces.

So, I no longer had any reason to take the scientific explanation of visionary phenomena seriously or to believe that I was on the brink of madness just because science mistakes a vision for a hallucination. Peyote had rid me of my greatest fear.

As I said earlier, I had no beliefs (even though the spirit of the cactus had sometimes carried me to the thrones on wings of fire), but having faith was possible once again: I asked for nothing more.

From then on, I knew that, in ordinary life, we only perceive the surface of things that we are suffering (why, I do not know) from a veritable case of *atrophy of the senses,* and that, under certain conditions, man can escape from the cell in which the inexplicable slumber of his abilities has imprisoned him.

Thus, I could also believe that we possess more subtle abilities in addition to those that link us to the physical universe. These abilities sometimes come to light and reveal, unbeknownst to ordinary consciousness, the spiritual entities and actions that Swedenborg, Blake, Rudolf Steiner, and other visionaries described.

2

LIKE A DRAGON ENTERS THE SEA

How does my name matter? It is wonderful.

JUDGES 13:18

One day, as I was walking down the path that ran alongside Thuret Park in Antibes, I saw a tall, blond figure arching its back in the wind.

Smooth white skin, like a woman's, clung to the cavities and gigantic bulges of its torso. Glistening beads of sweat ran down from the armpit to the stomach and the strong knee. Strong arms raised bended blades, which swished through the air, alternately showing their olive green and silvery sides.

I stopped in my tracks, stupefied by the perfect fusion of feminine grace and virile strength. You could say that the mystery that hovers over the union of man and woman had finally molded a body in its image.

This body had the majesty of old age and the svelte energy of adolescence.

Who was this being? What was his name? For a fraction of a second, I hesitated. The object of my contemplation seemed so much nobler than the name, which came to my lips, but I did not dare to apply it to him.

Then my error occurred to me: if I opted for the grisaille method, it was obviously impossible to name the regal hermaphrodite. There was too much disparity between him and that which I ordinarily called a tree or a eucalyptus tree. I was silently entering the sacred realm, deprived of a language that could only be applied to the profane. Like Joseph, I left the coat of many colors in the hands of Jacob's sons.

However, no one was forcing me to opt for the grisaille method.

I had the right to posit that I finally knew the true and Adamic meaning of words (at least the meaning of words designating things that presented themselves to my purified outlook).

Language, as the French poet Stéphane Mallarmé had already written, did not speak of that which man, banished from Eden, painfully continues to call a tree. Nor did language speak of an idea, like the philosophers imagined. Language spoke of that which truly is, that which is alive, that which is "really real," and that of the bare tree of the first days.

It was for this reason that mystics unanimously declared that the only ones who know the meaning of the word *God* are men who have *seen* him, and the only ones who know the meaning of the verb *to see* are those who were born of the Spirit, those whose eyelids have been touched by its marvelous finger.

It is also for this reason that the mystics tirelessly exposed the intellect's false beliefs. In fact, the intellect was not based on the "given" but was based on what our crippled senses mistake for the "given." It was on this wobbly foundation that the intellect was building castles of reason.

Of course, it was daring on my part to claim that just because I knew the Adamic meaning of the word *tree,* I also knew the Adamic meaning of the word *God,* or even that I could reply in the affirmative to the essential question.

However, the main cause for my skepticism had faded away. I no longer had any reason to doubt that the universe was exactly what language claims it to be: an order originating from the Divinity and at the heart of which man occupies a crucial place.

No longer having any reason to doubt, I doubted no more. I believed, just like one believes an oracle whose predictions have always come true.

A bird flew by, a leaf fell to the ground, and I could clearly discern the link between both these apparently distinct occurrences.

The prodigious refinement of my senses allowed me to see what linked them together. The air, put into motion by the living rocket boring through it, swirled around the leaf and plucked it off its brown stem with an invisible hand.

Thus, the link between both these occurrences was no different from the link between two colors in a painting or between the violin and the flute in a musical composition.

My perception was not extraordinarily different. It was only sharper, finer, and more extensive. Sharper in the sense that I had the time to see what generally escapes my attention; finer because it brought to light the tiniest nuances and the smallest details of each object; and more extensive because it operated in an infinitely wider sphere, which included the contours and structures of phenomena ordinarily hidden due to their small size and distance.

From the Garoupe Lighthouse towering over Antibes, I could

single out the haze of dawn between two peaks slowly descending in oracular silence into the Var Valley.

The sight was so *natural* that being able to enjoy it only under the influence of peyote surprised me more than actually being a witness to it. This wide river, dense, frothy, and white as milk, flowing in the wind's eye and loaded with iridescent clusters, reached the shady valley by solemnly unrolling its whirling waves. I obviously could not doubt that I perceived the river exactly like it was.

My perception contained no "imaginary" element. What I could have seen through a telescope was seen with the naked eye, the only difference being that a telescope, by magnifying objects, narrows the field of view, whereas I was enjoying the same panoramic view as I ordinarily did.

This also applied to the connections I could establish between seemingly separate incidents.

There was no difference between these connections and those that I observed daily. They were only more subtle and fleeting. The sharpness of my senses was, without doubt, wonderful. However, one can acquire this by practicing an art. I saw more colors than a painter did, and my ears captured more sounds than a musician's. The force and the flawlessness of my impressions alone were miraculous, and these impressions were inherently identical to those I received every day.

This in itself brought about the spiritual upheaval I endeavored to describe earlier.

In theory, the expansion of the realm of consciousness does not change the fundamental connection in any way. The obstacles and questions remained. Only the size of the chessboard and the shape and number of the pieces were new. In fact, the very meaning of the game was undergoing a radical change.

I discovered that the sacred was an extension and, if I might add, a spreading of the profane. It was hidden to those with eyes that cannot see and ears that cannot hear. It was the profane in full bloom.

In daily life, sensations seem to be enveloped by invisible cotton. I always feel less than what I would like to feel.

Sure, I might feel great pleasure in eating a peach; this pleasure is still inferior to the one that my imagination had anticipated.

No matter how piercing a sensation is, it almost never goes through the frigid space that surrounds the consciousness and isolates it from the world. I am truly touched only by exquisite pleasure and extreme pain, but this neither happens very frequently nor does it last too long.

I explained earlier that the real appears to be drowning in the unreal because of the numbing of sensitivity. It is also the insufficient reality of reality itself that encourages man to doubt language.

For a peyote enthusiast, even the slightest sensation is full and round like the stroke of a gong. It swamps the soul with its vibrations and only stops when the latter is full. As the expression goes, "One feels alive." A peach becomes an edible dawn; eating it is like diving ecstatically into its essence of freshness.

This shows how the peach holds all the promise contained in the images evoked by the word that designates it. There is no difference between the pleasure that these images foretell and the pleasure I actually get. I am completely fulfilled.

Also, my satisfaction is as spiritual as it is physical. Through the obvious act of eating a peach, I can verify the identity of the universal order and the verbal order. The peach is a concrete example. The figure made by the pebbles scattered on the road could represent anything: naked young queens riding on waves with their arms outstretched or flowing castles turned upside down by the stormy angels of the wind.

Looking around, I noticed that happiness was the principle of everything. At least, that was its human name. As I have written earlier, a more appropriate name would have been the Effluvium.

One could say that the structure of each object qualified happiness like an adjective qualifies a noun.

Over here, happiness was grass; over there, it was a tree; up there, it was blue, or radiant, or mobile and hazy; elsewhere, it turned brown and hardened, or was covered by scales, feathers, or fur; as a liquid, it rolled over the sandy beaches. . . .

It was always the same sight, but it was impossible to grow weary because each adjective gave an absolutely original and surprising meaning to the divine noun it qualified, like a genius at work, and each instant created a multitude of new expressions that, combined with those that preceded them, gave rise to more and more.

The vision of the divine nature purified me like holy water.

Its simplicity consumed the complexities of the intelligence and its countless and false discriminations. The most inaccurate was the difference between appearance and being, between the one and the many. The many do not hide the one: they reveal its essence: happiness. Happiness—that of things and my own—was being.

The unfurling itself was its nature. This unfurling was simply the spontaneous manifestation of its eternal exuberance. The universe was the laughter of being.

Of course, there was a difference, just like laughter is different from the mouth and like the facial expression is different from the feeling or the painting from the artist, but it was none *other* than the being.

The contradiction that intelligence had placed between the one and the many was an invention of the intelligence, and for this reason the difference could not be erased.

I, too, was an expression of happiness.

Just like it turned green in the trees and shone in the sun, so in man, happiness was understanding. The act of understanding was its human form. This was the meaning of the glowing serenity that illuminated my consciousness. I was different from other things in the same way that they were different from each other, by the possibilities inscribed in my structure; in my essence, I was one with them.

Before continuing, I find it necessary to describe in brief the change that willpower undergoes.

In truth, I do not know if this faculty exists. I want this, so be it, but the impulse fades away during the night. However, if one is talking, the use of words is necessary. The apparent clarity of the word *willpower* should suffice in our case.

A sensation enters the consciousness: we feel cold, for example. In daily life and for whatever reason, when we cannot act on this (by putting on a sweater or by turning on the heater), we have no other choice; shivering and chattering our teeth, we somehow tolerate a situation over which we obviously have no control.

Being accustomed to considering our sensations as external and thus independent of our will, we behave toward them while under the influence of peyote in the same way as in everyday life: we adopt a passive attitude. Also, because peyote amplifies sensations, when we feel cold, we feel like we are freezing.

Now, one can *act* on sensations—obviously, only to a certain extent—under the influence of the cactus; one can will oneself to give orders to the organism.

All one needs to do is to think strongly (*I want to feel warm*) and to follow the command, so to speak, like an eye following an arrow. Seconds later, warmth comes, and soon, because peyote is, like Michaux used to say, "excessive, extremely excessive," one sweats, languishes, and can take no more.

Often, at the beginning of a grand day, one suffers from superhuman and immense fatigue. The simplest of actions seems impossible. Immobility becomes a refuge. One would willingly quote Georges Danton if one had the strength to speak: "I have entrenched myself in the citadel of reason." However, the energy to open one's way out "with the artillery of truth" is missing completely; at least, this is what one believes. In everyday life, one could not really move if one felt similar fatigue.

Scholars—ever so quick to understand—base themselves on the silence and immobility provoked by this lethargic state and conclude that sometimes consciousness expanders plunge the subject into a "catatonic" state. Also, because the latter believes he is tired, he adopts a passive attitude and thinks he is unable to stand up, walk, or make any kind of effort, so he turns his attention to the movie in his mind and abandons himself to his inner demons, thus justifying the opinion of the scholars.

In fact, one does have the power to fight the fatigue. (Fatigue due to what, I don't know, but I think it is an established fact that almost all investigators suffer from it.) All one needs to do, once again, is to will, in this case, to think: *I can stand up; I am the master of my body.*

The muscles seem to be separated from one another, each one enclosed in its case, and they seem soft like wool, but above all, they seem far, far away. One cannot move them more than one can lift a range of mountains. Then one accomplishes an "act of faith," sends the command, and, like Lazarus, resurrects.

So, the attitude adopted by the investigator at the very beginning of the day is of great importance.

Peyote intensifies sensations, but it also enlarges the zone that willpower controls. Under its influence, we are to a certain extent less submissive to our organism and thus freer. We can chase away fatigue and other feelings of the sort like we ordinarily chase away tiresome thoughts from our mind.

Unfortunately, most investigators are unaware of this. It is imagined that peyote only affects the sense organs. This belief is probably the reason why so many narratives tell of terrible anguish.

Everyday life would not be so ordinary if I felt more, but, if more is paradise, too much is hell. Overcome with fatigue, I am easily convinced that more is already too much. Also, because peyote also enlarges the imagination, it is almost impossible for me to tell the difference between what is really happening and what could happen. The possible future—which means the *image* of what could happen if the sensations continue to heighten—is superimposed on the present and on the real and demonizes it. This color seems to hate me, this sound has claws and wants to tear me open, and this smell is sprawling over me to drain me dry.

Thus, it is mandatory for the investigator to understand that peyote changes his very being as much as the world does and gives him the power and strength to live in the new universe that his purified senses reveal to him. Instead of suffering, he must learn to call on the underlying energies in his organism and discover that these energies are at his disposal.

As the day progressed, I had to make an increasing effort to stay within the limits allowed by the inadequacy of my spiritual evolution.

Even so, I started to notice things that were not really extraordinary, but which seemed suspicious nevertheless, for they surpassed my innate abilities.

My gaze moved over the painting I was examining; the dark forms stood out; behind them were the lines of the original sketch. Each stroke of the paintbrush seemed isolated, as if suspended in a space between the chapped coat of varnish and the coarse surface of the canvas.

This vision was still "acceptable." At least it had been possible to control its accuracy. Here was a small dragonfly clinging to the yellowing tip of a stem. I admired its oval wings, encrusted with delicate veins, its long and slender abdomen ending in a clasplike appendage and its eyeballs shimmering like mohair.

However, I saw more than just the insect: I saw the fauvist halo that surrounded it as well, animated by a quick vibration. It seemed to me that its "vital form" was showing itself the concealed rhythm, which the vibrant dragonfly expressed.

The butterflies, honeybees, and wasps were inhabited by a similar rhythm. Flowers, too, had their own rhythm, as well as the plants—slower than that of the insects and of a slightly bluish tint. The trees were like beating hearts. A cat came out of a thicket and crossed the road, its head and spine swathed in glowing red, concentric waves.

I started to feel that all these rhythms emanated from the main rhythm of the Earth, which, in turn, was an emanation of the solar rhythm.

Each and every movement was a variant of the universal movement; each form was the symbol of the connection that the cosmos establishes with the being defined by that form.

The same movement was reflected through a multitude of countless forms, like the echo of the primordial *fiat lux,* and this movement was the pulsation of that Effluvium whose human name was joy.

I hardly noticed the limits of the powers I possessed. These limits were fluctuating and subject to my will. It was up to me to choose the limits in which I would remain.

If I wanted to fly, know the future, read other people's thoughts, even influence them, nothing could stop this, except that these desires were *irrational*. I do not mean that they are beyond human possibilities. I did not doubt that miracles were possible. I seemed to guess how the thaumaturgists worked the laws.

However, I had not gained the right to imitate them. I could visit the pure land, admire its wonders; I could not exercise the powers that I temporarily possessed without "tempting God."

The magic was linked to the nature of things. The universe was the *expression* of divine felicity: it was only an expression. It did not possess the being.

It resembled the Divinity like a portrait resembles its model. As lifelike as the resemblance might be, it is nonetheless a simple image. This is why magic was possible.

It was as simple for a thaumaturgist or a magician to manipulate the laws as it was for a painter to modify the distribution of the colors on a canvas.

In short, I lacked practice. I was incapable of working the laws like I worked the paintbrush.*

If I forgot that the peyote alone was upholding me, that the

---

*Here is the real reason for the accidents that sometimes happen and that cause much ado. Under the influence of peyote, I could only make "crazy drawings," meaning drawings that expressed in a clear, unpleasant, and morbid way the difference between my *intentions* and the *means* I actually possessed.

I wanted to draw the Buddha, and, in fact, I drew a fat man, grinning, with something grim about his serenity.

This obviously does not mean that nobody can draw a portrait of the Buddha. If I could continuously possess the strength and the liberty that peyote gave me, I would, in a few weeks or months, acquire the means that I lack and learn to draw like, for instance, Picasso.

Then I would learn to manipulate the substance like the sorcerers and magicians do. Accidents happen when the disciple confuses the "potentiality" with the "actuality," that is, as the scholastics would say, confuses what one can do in principle with what one can do in fact.

expansion of my senses was artificial, I ran the risk of succumbing to great temptation.

Something dangerous lay in wait for me: the danger of no longer knowing how to stop my gaze, the danger of slipping from abundance into overabundance and, with a sense of harmony, losing my mind.

When the effects of peyote reached their peak, one could, by crossing a diaphanous line, enter a world that was only too meaningful; a world that was inhuman because it was superhuman; a world too vast, too complex, too dense, and too bright, in short, a world so close to the central sun that its brilliance was unbearable.

To my left was a low, mossy stone wall, covered with ivy. In this wall, blackened and rusty iron stakes planted at regular intervals held up a wide meshed trellis.

On the other side of this grill was a trembling and buzzing bright red space above which clouds of spun glass floated, connected to the ground by ligneous offshoots.

I stopped: my gaze accidently fell on the wall, focused on a lizard. I began to "play" with it.

In truth, it was a strange game. I captured the lizard with a thought that it could understand: "I am stronger than you are, faster than you are. You are trapped, but . . . I am not sure that you are good enough to eat."

The lizard understood. Frozen in electric stillness, it raised its cruel head, ready to dive into a crack in the wall should I show the slightest sign of distraction.

Between its short, thick, muscular feet, a bag of greenish parchment throbbed. I admired neither the beauty of the lizard nor its turquoise livery of lapis lazuli, but the perfect combination of fear and efficiency.

The creature was trapped, it knew it was trapped, and it was trembling with horror. Nonetheless, it was absolutely alert, tensed like a bowstring. I gently let go of my mental grip. A crevice swallowed it.

I was at the oceanfront with David. A storm was rising. One could say that the spirit of the Gothic was playing in the thunderclouds.

Suddenly, a legion of young, naked men holding strong, dazzling, triumphant swords superposed the movements in the sky. They were "angels" or "gods," but they were totally imaginary.

Did their untimely appearance rouse slight irritation?

The fact remains that my gaze went far beyond, exactly like one shifts one's attention to avoid seeing something.

I shifted my gaze to the stellar system, as if it was the most natural thing to do. Beyond the bluish veils surrounding the Earth, in the primeval darkness, the constellations burned. There, meeting the sun of all suns, were The living of the abyss.

Their life was happiness, their happiness was action, their action was word, and their word was *life*. "And these beings came and went, just like lightning" (Ezekiel 1:14).

That evening, I reread Ezekiel. It seemed clear to me that the prophet had expressed this unity of all the workings by the vision of the wheel. However, something peculiar about the expression troubled me.

Ezekiel said of the four living creatures, "Each of them had the likeness of a man." He would immediately add, "Each one had four faces; and each one had four wings." Which human being could recognize the "likeness of a man" in such monsters? Ezekiel, in order to describe the angels, might have needed to use images and comparisons, thus making crafty use of language.

I was once again before the obstacle I had been trying to overcome since childhood.

Whether the vision of the angels was real or not, my mind uplifted to a wonderful image, which I could not describe with human language.

Not that language was flawed, but, being a mirror, it showed each person his own face. My own experience was so dissimilar to the common experience that I could only talk in an allusive or symbolic manner. More accurately, I could, to a certain extent, throw some light on the intellectual fundamentals of the vision, but due to the very nature of language, I was prevented from communicating its beauty and grandeur when in fact it was precisely this beauty and grandeur I wanted to speak about. You need to have felt it, and no longer doubt it, in order to admit the possibility of a miracle.

I had a secret, nevertheless, and the weight of this secret made me a lonely man.

Only those who carried around the same weight understood me: other visionaries or other madmen.

I did not feel like I had violated the divine laws. Peyote had, on the contrary, taught me to respect them, even though I understood them in a totally different way than did the churches.

However, I had been punished. I had seen "that which man thought he has seen," and now I had to bear the indelible memory of my dazzling experience like a burn mark.

Hasnamuss.

The mirror showed me two faces: that of the weak and fearful man I was becoming who hid his insignificance behind his dark obsessions, and that of the man I could become, if I became aware of my "nullity," as Gurdjieff would have said, liberating myself of my false worries and my frippery and accomplishing an essential transformation.

I contemplated the already worn-down tightrope walker; his dotted red nose moved forward with arrogant and stupid sensuality.

This tightrope walker had a "thinker's forehead" that fooled no one because his ideas were insignificant and fragile like insects beneath a shining carapace. His cheeks were surprisingly soft and feminine, like the cheeks of a rich old maid; he had a greedy and invasive mouth, designed only for extracting from things and words (oh, how the mouth loves words!) their savor, and a jaw that expressed stubbornness, but only the passive kind, capable of refusing things.

Something primitive or cruel, I'm not sure which, like a saurian light, bathed the lower half of his face, giving him an expression that contrasted with the dreamy and mocking expression of his gaze— this fleeting and fearful gaze, fragile as a flower, which looked everywhere, yet never found a foothold or certainty or consolation.

At any other given point in time, I would not have been able to bear the teachings of the honest mirror.

However, peyote not only did not give me the power to see myself as I really was, it also did not free me of insidious, almost involuntary indulgences. It did not relieve me of this light, impalpable, yet impenetrable mask that we always put on instinctively when we are faced with our own reflection, a mask that allows us to believe that we are "all the same," a little like what we want to be, that things are not so bad "after all," that we do not run the risk of "really" becoming the horrible clowns that we already are and have been for a long time. . . . Peyote not only gave me the power to see this but the courage as well.

Indeed, on a grand day I would not sport my usual face but the other one, the one of the man I could still become if I made the strict and indispensable effort to curb my pettiness. To put it more clearly, I would sport the "cosmic face" that would necessarily be mine if I reached the liberating limit.

In a way I was united with my future, and even though this union was temporary and uncertain, I could consider the present without trembling. I could measure the distance that separated me from my goal and the obstacles barring my way.

However, I did not consider that what was true for David and for me (I clearly saw that beneath the "cosmic face" of my friend was an "eternal adolescent" mixed up with a strong and dangerous animal) was also true for all men and that the other men possessed as much weakness and as many vices as I did.

This is why, on the day of my initiation, their aspect confused and disturbed me.

I neither wanted to nor could believe that men were like the creatures that peyote showed me, and I looked for an explanation that would allow me to safeguard the noble and pure image I had of humanity from being dragged in the mud.

Debarred from society for a million reasons, incapable of holding an honorable and useful place in the world, an object of suspicion for some, despised by others, I had been stuck in a battle for years.

It was tempting to think that beneath the image—so beautiful and pure—I had consciously created of mankind, another one was hidden, imprinted with the deformity of hatred; now, it was this subliminal image that superimposed its hideous colors on the true aspect of mankind.

However, this "objective" and "scientific" explanation would not suffice.

Thanks to peyote, I would simultaneously see what life did to me and to the free and strong man inside, to the seed, in other words. David also had this hidden potential waiting for the opportunity to bloom.

It was not long before I realized, during my observation of the crowd on the beaches and in the streets, that this potential was in each one of us, just like it was in David and in me. This freed me of my doubt.

To quote the teachings of Gurdjieff and all the other masters, all of us are sick people. In order to be cured, one must become "like children," which simply means that we must become what we are, become conscious of the distance between our thoughts, emotions, and true aspirations and those that we manifest, fooled by the "father of lies."

Generally, what was harmful was the fact that normal evolution was brutally interrupted at the end of childhood.

An "individual" was grafted onto the child, an individual who not only ignored the child's existence (or pretended to ignore it), but who also denied and stifled it. There was no connection between the ideas of the "individual" (his religious, moral, and practical convictions, his "Hasnamussian" convictions and ambitions, as Gurdjieff called them) and those of his true being.

Within all men, a parcel of the divine fire shone like a diamond.

Surrounding this fire, crouched low in the darkness and imprisoned in the walls of its dungeon was the "true self," graceful and pure. Surrounding the "true self," the "individual" proliferated, resounding with sinister ostentation.

Unfortunately, it is impossible to describe the *horror* inspired by this sight because the disgusting doll was feeding on the living being like a vampire. One could say it was a machine being fed on life, like a car feeds on gasoline.

Autumn came. I was back in Paris, with its dark sky and cold weather. I tried to recount my experiences to certain friends, but I was soon forced to shut up.

They regarded me with suspicion and would change the subject of conversation as quickly as possible. They behaved with me in the same way as I had with David before I had consumed the peyote. They were afraid and dissimulated their fear beneath arguments, which did not fool me, because I had used the same arguments to dissimulate my own fear.

I took peyote less and less often.

I no longer experienced the joys of the first summer. I was absolutely alone in this dark city. There was no one with whom I could share my sensations and ecstasies. I was the only one seeing the splendid storm clouds and the wonders of God.

Sometimes (in my normal state as well) I noticed *colors:* waves of tight and rapid vibrations with a double contour like the one given to objects viewed through a piece of feldspar.

They formed a kind of ring around people, sometimes resembling a flame, sometimes an almond. The dimensions, density, and substance of the ring varied. It presented as pockets, holes, and folds, and as tears or scratches and stars like a cracked window.

It was like language, but it was active, luminous, and alive.

A swarm of hairy red granules held together by a kind of gelatin signified suspicion; a broad steel band whose external border was shredded like a sword signified contempt.

A drunkard stumbled along his way through the brown and viscous smoke; an obscene thought appeared in the form of an undulation that had the consistency of dishwater.

As for the invalids, the organ that made them suffer was stamped with a sooty black imprint encircled by leaden red pulsations.

The colors that expressed joy, love, happiness, and serenity very rarely appeared. They were blue, purple, green, violet, and pink. These colors had the soft and transparent opulence of precious stones, the delicate and subtle structure of flowers. A regular movement, like breathing, animated them.

I still expected a lot from art, but I wandered the museums in vain. I couldn't understand. The most ordinary human being was infinitely more fascinating than these paintings, which were the objects of absurd reverence. At least the human being was alive; although I was continuing to see only crippled people or iguana and crocodile heads. However, I no longer had any doubt. Under the mask, a suffering soul pulsed.

Under the influence of peyote, I perceived the "subjectivity" of others as clearly as if it were my own. I could no longer ignore the feelings of others any more than I would ignore what I myself felt.

I do not mean to say that I could read their thoughts. It was really their attitude toward life, men, themselves, nature, and so forth—their "music," so to speak—that revealed itself.

There was no way to ignore it. It was not possible to not hear the music any more than I was not able to see the leaves stirring under my window right now.

This is probably one of the strangest "powers" that peyote gives. It effortlessly dissipates precisely that which makes the other, another; it blows away the fog and the darkness that ordinarily envelop the inner core.

Nothing remained invisible, hidden, or secret. I was not more separated from the inner world than I was from the outer world. Both these worlds were, in a certain way, on the same level. I could see an emotion pass by in my soul like I could see a bird fly in the sky, and I was surprised that I possessed this faculty.

I felt neither more insightful nor more intuitive than I usually did. It's just that a separation had disappeared, the one that I usually installed between the inner and the outer.

The effect a painting had on the person looking at it was as visible as the painting itself. Inevitably, this effect interested me more than the canvas causing it. In museums, I had trouble concentrating on the paintings: I was constantly distracted by pieces that were infinitely more complex, richer, and more surprising, which, strangely, had the reputation of being no more than frozen scenes hanging on the walls.

In the streets, people—at least sometimes—paid attention to one another. At the Louvre, their attitude was inexplicable; they concealed their boredom under abstract veneration. They were ashamed of feeling nothing; they attended service as if watched by a stern eye, careful to never miss a genuflection. Alas, God didn't hide in the dead paintings among which they halfheartedly and uncomprehendingly wandered, any more than he did behind the walls of the synagogues.

Because it was God, it was always God that people were looking for, without ever being able to find him because they were blinded by a false image that they had formed.

Their self-delusion was both exasperating and tragic. When they passed by a window, they hastened their step, holding their guidebook as if it were a missal. At times, I was filled with the dizzy desire to make a violent gesture, break the idols, tear down the paintings—almost all of them had been made by men who had *seen*—because no matter how beautiful they were, they only offered a pale reflection of the absolute wonder.

I myself had been an idolater for a long time. Now, it was difficult for me to believe in what each canvas was telling me. Van Gogh's were the most disappointing precisely because Van Gogh had obviously lived in that realm of energy into which I could only enter under the influence of peyote.

He had painted a just picture of this, but despite his genius, he could do no more. I always ran into this cruel fact, or more precisely, into this banality: a reflection of something is not that thing. Art is nothing, as the Westerners would say, but "a finger pointing at the moon." The exorbitant importance that we are currently giving to art is simply due to the fact that we mistake the finger for the moon, the sign for the signified thing.

The works of art expressed the understanding of those who had made them with sublime accuracy.

However, these men had long since gone to the Father. I could not join them. Thus, I was touched by Philippe de Champaigne's love for his daughter. How he loved her, and as for her, how she loved God! It seemed to me as if the girl was leading her father to the sky, transforming paternal love.

In front of this painting, I understood the famous lines of the German writer Johann Wolfgang von Goethe about the ascent of man through woman, celestial guide, and star.

At the Louvre, I only felt "at home" in the Egyptian sections.

I knew these princes with beaming smiles, these gods and these basalts. It was as if my feet were touching the soil of the country once again. Everywhere, I could read the signs of a prodigious history with which my destiny was linked.

It seemed to me that the red granite sphinx lying in its vault was filled with signs. The priests had weaved a net of epic poems around it. On its back and sides, a multitude of tiny, motionless black crosses floated, and in their cracks you could see crystalline effervescence.

A colossal amount of energy was stored up there. It was apparently used to make the mental voyage easier. If one ignored the beast and placed himself between its legs, a supreme wave would push the mind out of its physical envelope and carry it away into the altitude.

Straddling the sphinx, I climbed up toward a star. In front of the immense globe of golden color, filaments of brown and purple smoke pulsated.

At other times, I would stop in front of Sekhmet. A breath expanded the black breasts, and an opaline tear made eyeballs without pupils bulge out of their orbits.

I stepped back, wiped my hand across my face, and the vision was going into the stone. Then the mind slipped away, after a moment suspended in time.

Something like a sound halo formed itself around my temples. It was a closemouthed song without beginning or end, a rising sob echoing from abyss to abyss. The lioness seemed to be hearing it as well; her vacant gaze was turned toward a lost country.

Pharaoh held the handled cross, symbol of life, in one hand and a roll of papyrus, symbol of knowledge, in the other.

He was a great man among others, but the honors showered on him were legitimate; they were an expression of gratitude.

The people revered him as their protector. Pharaoh did not just defend the Two Lands from invasion, or should I say that this mission was just the temporal aspect of his veritable mission?

To men, he was the visible son of the gods, but to the gods he was also the intercessor and the guardian. He braved the ghastly dogs; he bore the burden of the shapeless, watery demon with numerous and obscene mouths. Under his double crown he was the master of space and death.

All those rocks were telling me that I was their new heir and that the very Flood had not broken an alliance older than the sun. Sometimes, forgetting reason, I abandoned myself with pleasure to vertigos and dreams from which I sprang like a fountain of youth.

I loved this place. The room received light from the high, arched windows. Scattered by the cold wind, the rain rolled down the windowpanes in livid lines, and these lines either widened or erased the traces left by the rain of the day before. Dark bushes and trees trembled in the garden.

I gradually discovered the greatness of the ancestors: they not only knew how to see, they also knew how to use the Substance. They possessed the science of the signs that alone guaranteed the domination of the magician against the unleashed forces. They knew how to give and take, knew the words and gestures, the oblations and sacrifices that allowed man to modify the circulation of the effluviums without disturbing the laws of harmony.

However, I considered with sadness the change that had taken place since the closing of the temples.

So I climbed a few steps and went through a few rooms—or a few centuries.

I stopped before a glass chest installed on a pedestal. There was a cinder block among the oblique shifts of reflections and other statues.

The worms had eaten the bottom of the robe, the hands were broken, and in the black and sinuous cracks, the twisted fiber of dry wood was visible.

However, the angel still shone through the ghost, and an immortal breath inhabited this body of smoke.

Standing before this statue, the very memory of my obsessions and anguishes disappeared. A vernal cheerfulness came over me. One could say that the yellow helmet of death had suddenly cracked, liberating a youthful head. The universal grass was bent under the marvelous knee of dawn, and the effacement taking place within me was also operating outside of me.

Egypt had spoken words of war to the abyss; it had conquered the abyss. The angel was smiling. The craftsman had given it grace; he had not given it strength. Of what use would strength be? The angel had no monsters to overcome, no abyss to go through. It was not even aware that there was an abyss. It was *here*. People walked to and fro; they were as grim as the day was dreary, and they stopped for a moment before walking on. The pitter-patter of the rain mingled with the rumbling of the cars. The angel was *here*.

3

METAMORPHOSIS OF THE BANAL

Years had gone by since my initiation.

I had read and reread studies that investigators had dedicated to consciousness expanders. I myself had tried to describe their effect several times. The result of my attempts always disappointed me.

I had never been able to really *say* what made peyote a sacred plant, in comparison to the fabulous soma of India, which even the gods consumed, as the Vedas say, "to maintain their divinity."

What is the obstacle I am referring to? I would like to examine this question now.

Let us imagine that I am describing any given place with meticulous precision.

Just by doing this I am giving the place importance and dignity, whether I want to or not. Indeed, I am not undertaking this task for no reason or "just for sake of it." My description obviously has a goal in view, which, as a matter of speaking, throws light on the things I am talking about like a lamp would, which intensifies their bulges and ridges.

The more detailed the description is, the more *dramatic* the illumination.

The place transforms itself and becomes the place of sublime or terrible events whose revelation must justify the accumulation of so many intricate details.

If I speak at length about this bush, the voice of God must burst forth from it.

Thus, trapped in the net of words, things only form the *setting* in which action must arise. They draw their interest from action, just like the sparks draw theirs from fire, just like the ardent bush draws its majesty from the angel inhabiting it.

So, in order for a description to be interesting, it is necessary for the author to have a precise reason to make it, a reason that justifies his insistence.

In *Toilers of the Sea* and elsewhere, Hugo has made great use of this process. For example, while reading the description of the Douvres cliff, one can feel that an extraordinary event is going to take place there. The short phrases, bursting with life, which seem to be on the verge of shattering under the pressure of their inner energy, give us the impression that Hugo can barely contain himself, that an incredible secret is pushing him, and thus, by conveying his own impatience, he renders the description irresistibly fascinating. A terrible threat hovers over every scene.

Hugo puts vocabulary of vertiginous wealth to the service of the "abyss," which unquestionably has a "peyotical" effect. Everything is recounted: the minutest details, the most fleeting nuances. Because these details and nuances are recounted, they are *magnified* in a certain way—in every sense of the word—enlarged as if they were being examined with a magnifying glass and glorified.

They are no longer just details; they are important, they have meaning, they are splendid and sinister, and they express this oscillation of the being between the divine *complexity* and the infernal *complication* that constitutes Hugo's universe.

It is obvious that the more one arouses the reader's curiosity, the harder it is to satisfy it.

The longer it takes for the mystery to be resolved, the more prodigious the event leading to it must be. However, *it is impossible, when one describes the world revealed by peyote, to satisfy the suspense aroused by this description.* The reader is inevitably disappointed. Needless to say, the things that the investigator sees are of extreme and exorbitant importance, but the reason for which these things are important eludes him.

Each bush contains an angel, but a closemouthed angel who confides no message, who dictates no law, and who is not responsible for the apostolate revealed to him.

In other words, it is possible to describe objects in such a way that the reader feels that, under the influence of peyote, these objects seem more beautiful, richer, and more enigmatic—in a nutshell, *more significant*—than they ordinarily do.

However, what is the signification that the objects acquire? What does it consist of? What is the "thing" that gives them this majesty and force? Instead of paying no heed to what we see, as we ordinarily do, why do we briefly glance in admiration and get the impression that we can contemplate objects eternally and that we are not before a laurel hedge, for example, but before the infinite?

It is possible to answer this question, but the answer is inevitably disappointing. In truth, the sublime and terrible events that the description announces are only *the calm exchanges that compose the universe at every moment.*

In everyday life, we know that the worst can happen at any given moment.

However, this knowledge is abstract, and we are not *touched* by it. When we are told of the numerous dangers that threaten us, we feel a lack of interest. This is common knowledge, and everyone knows it; no doubt, this knowledge affected us when we first acquired it as children, but it long since lost the power to disturb us.

In order to think about this, we must make a certain effort, which is quite painful and which tires us quickly. Toward this particular situation and toward this life that we lead, which is so constantly threatened and which continues nevertheless, we feel admiration and fear, both equally fake. Sometimes, before the starry sky, the storm, the mountain, we feel brief, albeit superficial, exhilaration, which disappears immediately.

Yet, the main effect of peyote (in my opinion) is to make us *feel* that which we ordinarily *think* we feel. Everything is possible. One no longer believes in the permanence of laws, in the necessary victory of order and harmony. Each step is an adventure. The dawn of every second is an absolute beginning, which gives the unlikely a chance to be. A tremendous force surfaces.

Under the influence of peyote, one can feel that heaven hovers over hell, just like the thin film on which man builds his cities hovers over the unknown. An omnipresent and furious energy, like the very face of war, meets the eye. The sun is an explosion;

the Earth, a conglomeration of titans frozen in the folds of their revolt.

One can ask if this perception is illusory, but if one thinks about it, it cannot be. For in the end, things really happen in this way. Whether we know it or not, whether we feel it or not, it is true that we are living at a crossroads of energies, and if we were always fully conscious of the inconceivable fragility of our existence, almost none of the questions that preoccupy us would have any meaning.

Thus, peyote removes the veil that *familiarity* imposes between nature and consciousness. The blind man does not see anything less than what we do; he sees differently, and neither he nor any peyote enthusiast can make us understand that we, who have always had sight, are suffering from blindness worse than his and that our indifference is scandalous.

In other words, peyote accomplishes a kind of *metamorphosis of the banal,* of that which we otherwise refer to as banality, because we fail to feel its essential singularity.

The metamorphosis is sometimes bleak. Concentric halos of anguish tighten around the investigator. A prisoner of the obvious, he sees that "all is abyss."* The sky sucks him up like into a hole; the horrible people in the cracks swarm beneath his steps. He cannot seek refuge within himself any more than he can outside. The truth is, his thoughts are not really his own. Between their source and the consciousness, the impenetrable throws its black arm. (Where are the words I am writing at this very moment coming from? By asking the question, I establish that all writing is "automatic" and that Breton simply defined what always happens.)

---

*[From the poem, "Abyss" by William Aggeler. —*Ed.*]

The investigator sees that he does not possess a "me" like he had imagined he did, that which the Prajna Paramita Sutras call a "permanent entity."

However, if anguish can arise from this sudden flaying of the mind, so can ecstasy.

It is awareness of this simple fact: the worst cannot happen. It certainly can happen, in a moment, but at this very moment—the only one that truly *exists*—the sky is blue, and I am breathing.

Thus, no matter what his attitude is, the investigator always has a keener sense of awareness of the universal and permanent miracle than we do.

However, he cannot share his wonder any more than the blind man I just spoke about can. Words are insufficient, and the lines I am writing prove this; they are only made up of words that, no matter how much I try, do not "speak."

If words had that ability that they precisely lack, the ability to tear us away from the "frail monster," from the demons of habit, then the man seeking relief in peyote would be crazy, for sure.

It would suffice to read, for example, *Toilers of the Sea* to become "like children." As paradoxical as this affirmation might seem, one of the fundamental causes of human unhappiness would be abolished.

There would be no difference between the world and its image as given to us by Hugo and all poets. At least the difference would not be *radical*. We would immediately see that men are just like Rimbaud describes them in "The Seated Men," in such a way that we would not be able to simply read, admire, and disregard. We would immediately feel the desire to get up and change.

Unfortunately, no image has the power to convince. It is always fragmentary by definition. An object's reflection only shows one of its sides. A shock is immediately followed by the memory of the shock. We are no longer struck by it; we admire it, and admiration is a cold monster that draws out the word *imaginary* from the word *image*.

4

H. M. AND THE GREAT WHIRLWIND

Dreadful faces are glimpsed in the gaps of the darkness. The descriptions are marvelous, but no matter how lively his curiosity (that insatiable curiosity was one of his most appealing traits), the profound antipathy the forces aroused in him remains.

All his books are a testimony to this antipathy. He did not suspect the malice of the forces. In addition to this, he seemed to believe that they regarded him with personal animosity.

Henri Michaux entered the rock. A tireless watcher, he ended up confusing himself with the gap. He observed, but also *criticized* (with all the hollowness of the word) relentlessly. In his journals, he minutely recorded the infiltrations of the shadow. Everything is lost except the writing.

He is *opposed*.

Opposed to men, opposed to things, but most of all, opposed to demons, spirits, gods, and God.

He easily gets rid of men thanks to the licensed H. M. process: the kneading. He obtains smooth, malleable, homogenous, and perfectly inoffensive dough; more than anything, he fears *intervention* (mine was quickly stopped). He forms a ball that he places on a wicker rack in the coolest corner of his basement.

Make a note of this: he *throws away* nothing; instead of getting angry, he leaves. Thrifty, Michaux.

He establishes less happy relationships with things.

Slyer, and therefore more dangerous than men, their "immobility," their "inertia" made for excellent camouflage.

One *forgets* them (one of Michaux's greatest fears). One walks on Insidious, follows Perfidy, bypasses Devious, smokes Pernicious . . . and one forgets! Just then, a pebble bounces into H. M.'s shoe, knowing exactly where to lodge itself in order to wound its victim's foot.

He was the fennec fox with admirable eyes, the sniffer and the smiler, sandy, and his paw was very delicately posed. . . .

This situation cannot *go on*. Fatigued, Delilah blended with Samson's substance. (The insomnia was visible from the start.) While waiting for the inevitable, he ruthlessly condemns the monsters' plots.

What about the mescaline? His attitude does not change. There are no differences between the works dedicated to his explorations of mescaline and the others. There are new characters, Mesc or Ha, obsessing him like the Bulgarians obsessed Plume.

He is attached to his critical thinking like a teenager who imagines that the devils get inexplicable pleasure from taunting him and intoxicating him in order to mock him.

He has an attitude that claims to be scientific: cold, impassive, and wary; it is, without any doubt, the worst attitude that a man desirous to visit the land of illumination could adopt.

On the walls of Balthazar's palace, one could see the mysterious handwriting of the words that religions had more or less explained the meaning of and whose tenets more often than not reflected their petrified caricature. However, for that to happen . . .

Let all will and desire and the most legitimate ambitions (especially the ambition of *knowing*) as well as the most justified aesthetic or moral preferences die.

Become a cloud, an element among the elements; subject yourself to all the suggestions of the force (yet, as we know, H. M. believes it to be malicious); the more docile, welcoming, and passive we are, the more profound and beautiful the experience. No more fear, no more curiosity, no more questions. Especially, no more questions! No matter how urgent they are (an illusion, by the way), do not allow them to enter the consciousness. If they somehow manage to break through, expel them immediately (but do it gently, otherwise the very effort will shake the soul in its deepest places and create a subliminal agitation, which is all the more harmful, especially because it has no detectable cause).

A "good mood" is indispensable, because under the effects of peyote, the world becomes a reflection of these moods. Fear gives rise to threat; hatred provokes ugliness; love arouses beauty.

Michaux's critical or "scientific" attitude inevitably provokes a "miserable miracle" and the rest. It is true that nowadays, in our society, the right attitude is very difficult, almost impossible to adopt (if I may say so). You are asking a man, an incarnation of the active principle, a Westerner (for whom this active principle is God himself) to take evil's side (or at least what the West calls "evil"), to make himself passive, feminine, Eastern . . .

Then, as we brush away the veil, we fear that we shall only find emptiness or, as Hugo would say, the shapeless space where the shepherd Vertigo guides the black sheep of hallucinations. We dread that the disappointment will take away what is left of the dim hope we take refuge in.

In his books about mescaline, Michaux only recounts the eventful moments of the battles he fought against the dragon at the threshold.

That being said, it takes genius to describe in the way he does an adventure that takes place entirely in this spiritual Antarctica, where the words of human language have never established more than temporary colonies.

The saints, the madmen, and the visionaries were all mistaken. It is totally possible to describe that which they have unanimously qualified as indescribable: this is what makes H. M.'s story so wonderfully interesting.

It is also true that it is an incomplete story; a beautiful map of the coast gives no indication of the inland region.

It is quite possible (and some indications allow us to think the following) that Michaux did not want to talk about all of this.

Before disembarking you need to be in the port, and for this to happen you must know the coast. No matter how cheerful the disposition of the man who takes mescaline, he inevitably sees the hideous reflections of his own anguish, reflections whose illusive character he does not recognize immediately.

We are too attached to this ensemble of habits, which we refer to as our "personality," to accept watching it dissolve in mescaline as if it were in a tub of acid.

The value of Michaux's testimony lies precisely in the obstinacy with which he defended himself against dissolution, thus giving horror the chance to display the complete range of its mirages.

Michaux has described the mirages in such minute detail that he has forever robbed horror of one of its main assets: *surprise.*

5

VISIONS AND HALLUCINATIONS

*Those who are in heaven are continually advancing
toward the springtime of life. . . .*

EMANUEL SWEDENBORG

In its simplest form, a hallucination arises when, for instance, we gaze at a wall and assemble its bumps, spots, and pits to form a face, which is always deformed and "Plutonian," as Hugo would say.

We are not fooled by these constructions, but one can very well notice how the essentially *organizational* activity of the mind superimposes itself on a sensitive subject. We see hideous faces, hunchbacks, and so forth in the bumps, spots, and pits, which we are always inclined to *humanize* and to draw out from their accidental assemblage, to create a form that we can recognize. We do the same in the case of a hallucination, turning one shadow into a mouth and another into an eye.

Yet, it is obvious that in the case of an authentic vision, if such a thing exists, nothing can appear that bears the slightest resemblance to the world as we know it, for the simple reason that an entity inhabiting the spiritual space does not need the same organs as we do.

In order to allow us to recognize it, the entity undoubtedly gives rise to an image and takes on a form that our imagination attributes to it, yet in its nudity, the entity has neither a human face nor a human body.

What do the following words mean: *expansion of the consciousness?* It is obvious that if it ever happens, I would not be able to witness it, because for that to happen, I should be able to observe that which observes within me. All philosophers have written that this act is impossible.

However, it is not necessary to observe that which observes in order to know that the dimensions of the conscious sphere are subject to variations.

For example, in my sleep I am only conscious of myself, even though the memories and worries of my subjectivity manifest themselves in a seemingly dispassionate manner, an illusion I am fooled by as long as the dream lasts.

Thus, the restriction of the conscious sphere to the "me" of the dreamer defines oneiric consciousness (according to a dualistic perspective, of course). On the other hand, during my waking state, I am conscious of the mental and emotional worlds. One can define vigilant consciousness by this expansion of the sphere in which its activity takes place.

Thus, it is understandable that, in certain circumstances, in ecstasy or under the influence of peyote, a new expansion takes place in such a way that the consciousness envelops not only the mental and emotional worlds but also that which contains them both: the world of natural powers. Also, it is understandable that sometimes, by transgressing a limit, the consciousness ventures into the spiritual world.

A hallucination is *defective* perception. For example, it happens when we take a curtain blowing in the nocturnal breeze to be a ghost.

We see less clearly than we ordinarily do, and thus we do not recognize the curtain. Hallucinatory phenomena are hence provoked by a weakening or a diminution of the basic capacities of the senses. They happen in the dark or when I am drunk or sick or half asleep, their cause being that my faculties are not functioning perfectly.

A vision, on the other hand, is *keener* perception. I am not more or less lucid than I ordinarily am. Far from taking the curtain to be a ghost, the visionary sees through the curtain. He does not suffer from diminution but, on the contrary, benefits from an increase in the capacities of the senses.

Still, this distinction does not allow us to define the essential characteristics of a vision in a totally satisfying manner.

It is important to add that a hallucination implies a certain *confusion of planes*. I hallucinate when I do not automatically and instinctively distinguish the mental space from the sensitive space, like I ordinarily do, as a result of which I have the illusion of seeing with my human eyes an entity or an object that is clearly the fruit of my imagination.

When I am in my ordinary state I can imagine a diabolical face: it does not frighten me, for I know that it is a creation of my mind, an occupant of the mental space. When I hallucinate, I forget this.

To me, it seems that I can see something rising up in the sensitive space, something that is not there. It is this deceitful acting out of the imagination that constitutes the ghost.

On the other hand, in the case of a vision, one maintains a perfectly clear understanding of the difference between the various levels of the being.

If one sees an angel, one can clearly perceive that it belongs neither to the sensitive space nor the mental space, but to what one might refer to as the spiritual space, for want of a better term.

Obviously, this term is totally inadequate, logically speaking, but I think it is quite clear. It is important to underline, once again, that the visionary is not less conscious but more conscious. He does not confuse the mental and the sensitive spaces; on the contrary, he clearly distinguishes one from the other. Furthermore, he distinguishes yet a third level, beyond these two, the one in which the activity of the being revealed by the visionary capacity takes place.

He does not project his imagination on objects; he perceives a reality that is beyond both his imagination and the objects.

He immediately perceives the characteristics that differentiate the angel from the beings subjected to terrestrial laws.

He immediately recognizes that something, which is revealed to him, can neither exist on Earth nor, as a consequence, can it be the simple image of that which exists on Earth.

A hallucination, on the other hand, takes place, as we have just seen, when, for whatever reason—fatigue, intoxication, or madness—the partition that separates the mental space from the sensitive space is removed, for example, when the spots spattered on a wall combine together to form a face.

In this case, the wall plays the role of the screen on which the imagination projects its faces.

During a hallucination, nothing except the content of the mind appears. *It is the manifestation of the impossible:* a familiar form (a face) surfacing in a place (the wall) where no being with a face can live. It is thus the negation of terrestrial laws. A madman is a man who believes that the wall can see him.

In everyday life, we doubt God's existence because there is not sufficient evidence to prove it.

On a grand day the evidence is, or seems to be, plentiful, so much so that doubting is no longer a possibility.

We do not doubt God as much as we doubt the right to doubt, which is created by ordinary consciousness. What is insufficient is not proof of his existence, but the capacities of ordinary consciousness.

This leaf is a leaf from the branch that my gaze spontaneously links it to, just like it links the branch to the trunk, the trunk to the roots, and the roots to the ground. Also, this tree is a tree from the sky in which it flourishes, from the clouds and birds filling the sky, from the hills, valleys, and other trees.

A hallucination thus arises when the intricacies of these connections are, for whatever reason, shattered.

If an object is removed from its natural place, it tends to separate itself from its name; it ceases to be that to which its name refers. A flying tree would no longer really be a tree. It would be a dizzying exception to the laws that we know and a destruction of the order manifested by these laws. It would be a marvelous being or a terrible being or both marvelous and terrible all at once—ambiguous, a negation of the mind.

Thus, a vision and a hallucination are linked: the visionary perceives more connections than the ordinary consciousness does, and the person hallucinating perceives fewer connections than the ordinary consciousness does. As for the ordinary consciousness, in a certain way it is both visionary and hallucinatory at the same time. It is visionary inasmuch as the ordinary consciousness perceives certain connections that the visionary perceives, and hallucinatory inasmuch as the ordinary consciousness denies certain others, which do not appear to the visionary any less than the initial luminous and undisputed connections.

In other words, for ordinary consciousness, God is a possibility that counterbalances another one: the absurd. However, this balance only lasts because the consciousness does not benefit from the faculty to perceive the divine order.

The visionary's world does not *deny* the ordinary consciousness's world, it *envelops* it.

You can see how these observations can apply to insanity.

The madman is a lunatic who believes that his perception is real, that the connections perceived by ordinary consciousness are illusory (in the same way that a "normal" man is a lunatic who believes that the connections perceived by visionary consciousness are illusory).

The madman does not think the absurd: he sees it; he experiences it. The hideous strangeness of things crushes him. A captive of the infinite machine, he only finds an outlet in suicide or murder.

Except, it so happens that the powerful organizer of the mind remains intact.

The madman perceives fewer connections than the ordinary consciousness does, but he perceives some of them. He lives in a mutilated world, but it is his world all the same. To come to terms with it, he uses his intelligence exactly like we use ours.

He works with an incomplete dictionary, in a manner of speaking, which is missing some essential words, thus leading to these deformed theories that allow him to explain everything.

However, it is important to point out that these theories are not very different from our own.

For a man who has taken peyote, the differences between them tend to fade away. Some are poor; others are rich. They all seem incomplete or presumptuous to him, including those with differences he could point out based on his own vision.

Nothing, for that matter, can guarantee that this vision embraces the All. Maybe certain forms of consciousness exist that would consider his perception to be crippled, just like ordinary consciousness is to him, and just like a madman's consciousness is to ordinary consciousness.

He comes to an outlook similar to the Eastern one, in which the entire universe is a hallucination because each perceived order implies one and then another that is vaster and more complex.

6

THE LAND OF ILLUMINATIONS

It took about an hour for the peyote to mix with my blood.

However, the very act of taking peyote almost always created a shock to the system. In big or small doses, it made me another man; the substance that I had just consumed isolated me from my fellow creatures, as if I were a sick man infested by germs.

I felt nothing. To be more precise, *I could feel that I felt nothing.* The joints of my body, the weight and the warmth of my clothes, the play of my muscles, the slumber of my bones, the imperceptible breeze aroused by my movements—all these insignificant things had acquired a peculiar character.

Why peculiar? This remains a mystery. These things remained insignificant; yet, my attention had trouble leaving them alone, and not without regret.

The glass on my table was still a glass, but because I looked at it differently, I saw it differently. Enclosed in blue silence, it spread a range of lunar strips on the tablecloth.

I paced up and down. Seated, I thought of sleeping; lying down, I thought of getting up. More than ever, I wanted to act on something, "do something." Brief spells of dizziness ran through my body. My stomach hurt.

I knew that the American Indians held these signs to be beneficial. Christ began by driving away the bad spirit, which needs to be vomited by the adept before the peyote—"Christ's gift to the red man"—can take effect.

It is necessary to be pure in order to cross the threshold of the pure land, and for this, it is necessary to pass through the purgatories that guard the doors. . . .

I admired the American Indians, their indifference to the plant's taste, to the anxieties and the nausea that accompanied the intake of peyote. I remembered old Chief Yellow Hand, who, one day, in order to prove his courage to the young men of the tribe, consumed forty cactus flowers and disappeared, without leaving a trace.

I felt nothing except a black and elated ascent from time to time.

The approach of drunkenness can give us an image of what this phenomenon is like, but only a rough image, because wine is only the colorant of the soul, whereas these energies seemed *conscious*.

I felt that I possessed an intelligence that was different from my own and indifferent to my own, an intelligence that was powerful and pursued unfathomable ends.

I was not being held by a substance, but by a force that was faceless and shapeless, a malignant mist that suddenly melted away into the shadows from where it came, leaving me attentive, my chest trembling.

Sometimes, when the uneasiness became too strong, I would close my eyes. That is when I perceived the "Mexican faces." Green and rushing by, they were just like the forces I was abandoned to by this bitter powder, which seemed like a dream and a grave.

I had saved some of the leftover, crushed, and rotten bone remains in my cupboard that the American Indians refused to sell, infinitely more precious than these blackened, waxen, heavy, and obtuse turquoises. . . .

I had eaten some of this bone powder, some of this terrible-tasting gravel. Why? It was always the same story: I always had a good reason before I did it. I wanted to "understand" as well as confront the worst, put my courage to the test. Then, when it was done, it seemed to me as if it was somebody else who wanted to "understand" and that this other person was mad.

I closed my eyes and looked at the Mexican faces.

I saw a heraldic serpent, in stone, with signs running all over its sides, a flat snake whose tight scales formed a decorative frieze.

I could distinguish cracks and holes; the stone was red, with yellowish veins, flaky and worn down by the wind and the centuries.

The signs appeared on the left, went down, turned, went up, turned, went down again, and finally came out at the right side of the visual field.

The language was one of energy: suns, crosses, squares, swastikas—a movie for sorcerers. Sometimes, I understood it. For example, the swastika represented a nebula—the decisive explosion of the great beginning. However, even when I did understand it, it was useless.

The faces came alive: crocodiles, abysmal flowers, toothy vultures with skull necklaces. The movement became faster and followed the same sinuous path relentlessly, but it seemed to me that this path had come to life. It was like the crawling of the primal clay.

The forces appeared from time to time. During the intervals

I continued to feel that I felt nothing. The universal insignificance exhausted me. It was like abstract torture, without discernible content.

However, I could recognize the initial effects of peyote. Albeit minute in appearance, they transformed my relationship with the world, little by little.

An endless number of *details,* to which I habitually paid no attention, invaded my field of perception.

I looked through the window: a shining or dark sky appeared. However, I could not ignore the fact that I was contemplating it through the traces left by the rain on the windowpanes and the specks of dust that tainted their transparency.

If I looked at these traces, they became more numerous, diverse, and complicated. I could distinguish the opalescence and ocelli of the glass.

I perceived nothing—or almost nothing—that I was not capable of ordinarily perceiving. (This is why the description of objects seen under the influence of peyote is so deceiving: one only describes them like a meticulous observer would.)

The difference was that I could no longer exclude from my consciousness the things toward which I did not voluntarily direct my attention.

The instinctive choice, which usually presided over the order of my perceptions, no longer functioned.

I could no longer make the parts dependent on the whole or the least important—what I considered as the least important—the most important.

The new abundance of details and the insistence with which they solicited my attention revealed the innate strangeness and the *inhumanity* of things to me.

The windowpanes and the stains spattered all over them had a life and a destiny of their own, as did the hazy spirals coming out of my pipe. The chairs and the table led an existence that their names did not reflect.

To me they were chairs and a table, but only to me. Their role—the one that man imposed on them—was not to be confused with their being-ness.

Stopping before a pile of stones, I no longer perceived the pile; I perceived the stones.

One was lined with lichen, another one was coated with an oval-shaped tear of dusty tar, yet another one was shattered and sharp edged.

Some of them were bound by absurd affinities and formed groups; others, originally from the same rock, bore a family resemblance. Each one wore an expression like no other: dishonest, obtuse, sardonic, coarse, and beaming.

Their unique expressions seemed insignificant to me, insofar as I remained true to human nature, and I considered them to be details.

However, the fact that a stone had a particular shape and a story inscribed in its pits and folds had its own importance in the stone's world.

I had more and more trouble denying this. The effort I needed to make was more and more exhausting. As soon as I let myself go, I would start to examine details, which I considered from the stone's point of view.

From then on, these details would multiply and grow; they were innumerable: they reached out to me in the crystalline daylight with fierce stubbornness.

Strictly speaking, I did not believe that objects had the consciousness required for the constitution of a world.

The consciousness that I attributed to them was no different from the one I attributed to the forces.

For this consciousness, the stones, the smoke from my pipe, the furniture in my room, the stains spattered on the windowpanes, and the movements in the sky had a life and a destiny of their own independent of man. It was this consciousness that impugned human nature and conferred on the details, as I would call them, an inexplicable dignity.

This consciousness knew nothing about our values. More accurately, the very concept of values was unfamiliar to it. It was the eternal contemplation of an infinite swarm.

It was as if peyote was urging me toward this contemplation. Feeling the objective insignificance foretold the invasion of my mind by the *other* one—a mind that knew nothing about differences, not even between sense and nonsense.

Above all, I recognized the change in myself by the change that the appearance of the clouds underwent.

Vitreous layers rolled one on top of the other, rapidly and silently.

Dark veins meandered within these layers; their crossings formed a sort of fishnet with round stitches, which the winds widened and tore apart.

Sometimes, a hyaline abundance sprang up. A ray of sun would pierce through it, surrounding the bulbous contours and illuminating its core.

Even though I removed my glasses, I continued to see the inside of the clouds. However, my vision was blurred; the lines split in two and trembled; white asterisks invaded my field of vision.

I remained impervious to the altitude.

In order to like it, I needed to attain the "luminous side" of the peyote. As long as I stayed on the "obscure side" no sight had the power to touch me.

My indifference upset me. I tried to lift the iron cover that was suffocating me. The vanity of my efforts irritated me.

Things seemed to constrict and harden, as if my looking at them had burned them. However, I perceived, more and more acutely and painfully, their cracks, their aging, and the shadows that clasped them like bloody claws.

Suddenly, an essential nakedness rose up in my consciousness. It was toward *me* that the thing was heading. The approaching danger I had sensed a few minutes earlier was lurking over my body and my mind.

The light was tearing me apart. All exits were closed. I had no time to prepare myself for the encounter. I had to answer the questions that the stranger was asking me here and now.

These questions were the simplest ones: Did I have the strength to live? To love? They mingled with the odors I was breathing in, with the sound of the wind, with the sap trapped under the varnish of the wooden floor, with the swaying of the curtains. I was leading a battle against a dark power.

The object was losing what made it an object: its passivity. A messenger of the dark power, to me it appeared like a balloon distended by a strange breath. Its uneven and gleaming surfaces showed themselves to me; I watched out for the snapping of the stitches that held them together.

It was more and more difficult to believe that this was a hallucination.

It could only be one if the meaning that man gave to things was truly their meaning, not just a kind of clothing to dissimulate their futility, like modern consciousness tends to do.

It was a hallucination in the sense that I attributed a consciousness and aggressive intentions to the absurd.

However, the convictions of reason were losing their strength. Behind the sense and the nonsense, the *antisense* was emerging: a nature that was foreign and demonic, an active refusal of human nature.

One could say that peyote revealed the hostile principle to me, which ordinarily man only knows through the harm inflicted on him.

The opposition of good and bad was an illusion. It was an illusion because the good was an illusion, the dream of ignorance and hope. Only the bad was real.

Its face was ugliness and suffering, eternal and infinite suffering, which things took part in, like I did. The chair had an unsteady shine to it; the red of the cushion pulsed like a burn wound; the folds of the carpet had something painful about them; the sound made by the open tap elicited the feverish throbbing of a migraine. The universe was suffering from a gigantic illness whose countless symptoms I could not stop seeing everywhere.

The attention that I accorded to this illness varied according to the circumstances, and especially according to the position, I found myself in.

The illness often appeared in the form of an inexplicable desecration, but it was rare to attain the "luminous side" without going through this darkness.

No matter how much I told myself that I was projecting my own craziness on the world, the desperate thoughts whose fascination I, like most of my peers, was subjected to revealed the obvious.

I was vainly seeking a sanctuary within myself. I was disgusted by my body. It was covered in grime, sweaty and swollen with nasty juices.

The saliva, which my tightened throat refused to swallow, was rolling over my tongue. The bones in my skull stifled my brain; the convolutions of my brain stifled my mind.

If I stood up, I was unsteady on my feet; if I sat down, the edges of my chair dug into the hollows of my knees and my shoulders; if I lay down, I could not stand the heat and softness of my bed.

I went outside. The street was wider, and the houses were taller. Wind and fog rumbled in the evil yellow sky.

A halo of vibrations surrounded the slightest sound: the creaking of a shutter, the crunching of gravel, the purring of an engine. The hunchbacked cars passing by seemed to engulf the street; from their smooth posteriors decorated with bright protuberances, gases escaped, panting obscenely.

The cracks in the sidewalk got deeper and branched out. Their chapped lips concealed mossy pebbles, as if they were fossilized. Rust encrusted the gutters with sharp red blotches.

I walked next to walls with wrinkles like old bellies and covered with fluttering rags. Everywhere there were stains, smears, streaks of bird droppings, and puddles. Newspapers lay dead in the corners.

The people were especially frightening. Not only because their appearance was hideous, but also because through this I could see the tremendous change operating within me, as clearly as if I were looking into a mirror.

The hollow bystanders gave me looks that were full of hatred, or they would stiffen and ostentatiously display their colossal indifference.

Where were they going? What were they doing? Who were they? I was surrounded by inscrutable machines that were permanently going down the rails of madness.

A man was walking in front of me. Stirred by the wind, the hem of his overcoat flapped about with effeminate grace.

One would have thought that under each boot he wore a spring, which gave his steps a metallic staccato.

The back of his head was rawer than it was bare, sculpted in flabby and pink flesh, which formed a roll of fat at the neck, from which yellow hairs dangled. His tiny hat seemed to be sucking at the top of his head.

The break of dawn, sudden and irrefutable, marked the end of an ordeal.

The change affected the past as well as the present; not only did I stop fearing the demons, I also stopped *having* feared them. It was not I that they had tormented but someone else, a sleeper whose memory was blurred with that of the dreams that had visited him.

I could *understand*. So what? The question seemed ridiculous at the time. Like Rimbaud, I exclaimed to myself, "It's too beautiful! Let's keep our silence." A spiritual light indistinctly bathed the immensity of the knowable.

The anguish had disappeared, along with its cause: the crucifying opposition of the human order and the natural order. Their union formed a new and sublime order: divine. It was this order that my contemplation revealed to me.

The details were as numerous and diverse as during the ordeal.

However, they no longer contested the meaning of the object. The tree was a tree from the tip of its roots to the tip of it leaves; the day was the day in its most shadowed recesses and gilding.

7

PEYOTE UNIFIES THE BODY AND THE WORLD

Sometimes I would enter the peyote like a dragon enters the sea. At the time, the experience would begin with a progressive deepening of the sentiment of the beauty of things. The forces showed themselves only in the form of prismatic efflorescence.

Most often, as I've already said, the waiting was long, dreary, and irritating. Only the increasingly unbearable awareness of the universal insignificance double-crossed the effects of the peyote. I was in a world that was gray, woolly, as tasteless as stale water, and banal—*strangely* banal, but here, in my opinion, is an important point.

My inner state was different from my usual state only because I was unable to drag myself out of it. I was unable to distract myself, unable to look for solace in my ordinary occupations, like reading or walking or dreaming or working. I was unable to look for that temporary oblivion of everyday life that, in fact, veils its paucity.

Every second of the way, I was compelled to live with this

indigence, which, ordinarily, my activities would force back to the confines of consciousness.

What does *banality* mean? Why does man attribute a negative connotation to the term he uses to designate the very basis of existence?

It seems to me that the only possible answer is that banality generates boredom and that boredom is a form of *anxiety,* an anxiety lacking color, so to speak.

If I am unable to fix my gaze on objects, it is because their bottom is too close to their surface for me to find durable satisfaction in contemplating their details.

This observation is frightening because it means that language is a liar, that things are not what language announces them to be: full of spiritual treasures, capable of satisfying the hunger eating away at me, which yearns for an object of eternal contemplation.

This is how banality expresses, in an indistinct way, a possibility that modern consciousness has made a certainty: if visible and tangible things are not what language announces them to be, then invisible and intangible things are not either.

If this rose—this "queen of flowers"—is nothing but a scented ball of petals surrounding reproductive organs—pretty, no doubt, but indignant at having been the center of attention for only one moment—how can I believe that the "big words," as we rightly call them, are not even more misleading and that they do have a real meaning, a substance, other than the vague images they fill the mind with?

One can now, I believe, make out why the initial effects of the peyote were so alarming.

It began with an *involution* of the significant power of speech. Death was invading the world because life was withdrawing itself from language. The yellowing flowers, branches, and grass were nothing more than what they appeared to be. They no longer had even the little meaning that they ordinarily did. They were there, crouched down abjectly in their shady puddle.

Then the expansion of the conscious sphere began. Unbeknownst to me, *I was losing the ability to tell the difference between what was happening within me and what was happening outside of me.*

The anxiety worsened as the loss of this ability manifested itself.

I was no longer lodged in my organism as if in a moving fortress and protected against the universal violence by the density of my flesh and the strength of my bones.

The sounds that lashed my ears, the forms that filled my view or swarmed under my fingers, and the flavors and smells did not seem farther away from the center of my being than the organs that allowed me to perceive them.

I felt a plane fly across the sky as if I were feeling my own eyeballs moving in my eye sockets. The rumble of its motor affected me in the same way the beating of my arteries did. *Peyote unified the body and the world.*

I could no longer distinguish my emotions from my sensations; neither could I distinguish the sensations produced by exterior things from those produced by my liver or my intestines.

What happened to me happened to the world, and what happened to the world happened to me.

From this confusion the strange and deformed were born as if from the abdomen of Chaos. The chair shared my anxiety and thus was not a chair, no more than the sick table was a table and the astonished cushion a cushion.

What names should we give them? The question simultaneously worsened my anxiety and theirs.

The "subjectification" of the sensitive space corresponds to the "objectification" of the mental space. If the chair shared my anxiety then my mind had the fibrous consistency of wood and the yellowish shine of straw.

Not understanding the unifying action of peyote, I felt as if I had been hit at the very core. I keenly defended my "me" against a multitudinous invasion. The "other" who oppressed me manifested itself in the form of black and jubilant forces.

If the forces seemed to have a personality, it is because I refused to surrender mine to them. Their personality seemed dangerous to me, diabolical even, because it demanded such a sacrifice from me.

The fear of an essential change showed itself, like in a mirror, in the form of the threat whose target I believed I was.

The more scared I was, the closer the overhanging threat became. I could banish it only if I did away with the cause of my fear: this attachment to the "me" was the bad spirit that the American Indians exorcised by vomiting.

I certainly did not need to take peyote to know the ugliness of mankind and suffer from it.

However, I was suffering now as if I had worn this humiliated flesh myself. Paradoxically, it was because I did not feel different from other men that I questioned their humanity.

If they were like me, they would suffer from their ugliness and vulgarity like I was suffering. Not only did they seem to tolerate it, they also found it natural. They shamelessly spread out their jowls and bellies. They precisely loved that which horrified me. If this was what men were, I was not one.

Because my reason was intact, I kept the power to attribute

the transformation of my attitude to the influence of the peyote. However, like we have seen, I could no longer find an ally in my reason. The disruption I was going through explained my darkest thoughts.

In a way, hallucination was more truthful than what is called normal perception. It had revealed the emptiness of language to me. If a chemical substance altered things to a point where it was impossible to name them by their names, then language was a toy. I was experiencing that which I had only thought about so far: an agony and crucifixion of speech.

I did not know for sure that men were my fellow creatures; I could only *believe* it, and, yet again, in order to believe it, I had to believe in language.

I was in a situation similar to that of the French philosopher and author René Descartes: "What do I see from the window beyond hats and cloaks that might cover artificial machines whose motions might be determined by springs? But I judge that there are human beings."

Judgment is an act of absolute faith. Descartes had only *thought* of this act. He had doubted everything except maybe the very basis of Western philosophy: the similarity between thought and being, admitted from the time of the ancient Greek philosopher Parmenides.

I discovered that *thinking* that men are human beings had no effect on my anxiety. As long as I did not *feel* it, my judgment remained abstract. It was an intellectual act, a fake one.

Then, the conversion of anguish into joy would take place, which marked the end of the ordeal.

This conversion would happen when I abandoned myself to the

invasion of the terrible thoughts that tortured me instead of fighting against them.

Suddenly the strength and courage to reject them was missing. I allowed myself to fall into the abyss. Immediately a gentle force would uplift me and carry me over to the other side.

The ordeal went on for three hours at the maximum; I would spend about ten hours in the light of the divine order. However, according to me, the anxieties and joys of peyote come from the same source, in such a way that the explanation for some of them is applicable to the others.

Like a friend would say, "Supreme ecstasy is identical to supreme fear: the only difference is that in ecstasy, one *knows* it."

My emotions and sensations were confused. However, now I abandoned myself to this confusion or, more accurately, to this fusion, and it was this acceptance that operated the metamorphosis.

Peyote has erased one of man's biggest illusions—the illusion of solitude—because the body and the world are indeed one: I only know them through the messages that my nerves receive. The difference I make between them is abstract.

I do not see that tree, but rather its image that my optical system sends to the brain. I do not touch it either: this dry and rough sensation is, in fact, a tactile image transmitted by the epidermis to my brain.

If I touch tree bark, it would be perfectly legitimate to say that, by touching, I know some properties of my organs. (Philosophers would go further and say "of my mind.") It is not any less absurd to mistake an object for the messages that my senses send to me than to mistake a letter for the person who sends it.

These observations seemed to justify solipsism. If I only know the properties of my organs, then the universe is my dream and the other human beings are only ghosts inhabiting the dream.

However, this interpretation neglected the essential fact that *a universe populated with ghosts is not a human universe.*

The universe, which peyote revealed, necessarily contained consciousnesses that were similar to mine and to other different animal or angelic consciousness. I could communicate with them like I communicated with the trees and the waves in the sea because the possibility of this communication was inscribed in my structure.

How do I know the object? I found it useless to look for an answer to this question: it is asked only because the dualistic illusion is more powerful than the knowledge of oneness.

Knowing that it is my imagination that puts distance between my body and the world is not enough; I do not *believe* it. As long as I do not believe it, that is to say as long as I do not *feel* it, the knowledge I can have of oneness remains abstract.

Peyote gave a tangible substance to this knowledge. It erased dualism. From then on, I have never asked myself about an object's nature.

The messages that I received from my senses fully satisfied me. I no longer tried to decipher the mystery of others through these messages. The other was an intellectual ghost. What mattered were the messages, not the imaginary object from which they emanated.

I was no longer a human body in an inhuman world.

The dry and rough sensation I perceived when I touched tree bark was no less human than my feelings and thoughts. It was impossible for it not to be, since the organ through which I perceived it was a hand.

In this way I could extend qualities that I ordinarily only applied to the movements of subjectivity to this sensation.

Just as the world had participated in my anguish during the ordeal, it now participated in my bliss. As for me, I felt immense, like the world, and full of mysteries, just like it.

8

QUETZALCOATL

According to me, the most striking representation of the relationship that man creates with the universe under the influence of peyote is the one that is offered to us by the Mexican sculpture whose reproduction was displayed about four years ago, I think, at the Petit Palais: from the massive base formed by its stacked-up rings, the head of a feathered serpent sprang out, and in its distended mouth the face of a noble and serene warrior appeared.

For a peyote enthusiast, such a work of art could only represent one thing: the absolute *fact*, expressible and indescribable all at once, to which he was suddenly initiated (or "initiated," because an artificial expansion of the consciousness is necessarily temporary).

The human and the inhuman are not opposed, as the dualistic mind imagines them to be; I come from Quetzalcoatl just like a fruit comes from a flower.

First of all, this means that we are not *created* in the Jewish sense of the verb. God did not "freely" decide to make mankind one fine day, and the inevitable question is why.

Second, human consciousness is not the daughter of chance. It would be interesting to show that although modern and "scientific" in appearance, this explanation of the Beginning is, in the end, identical to the other: if God creates, that is to say, if he intervenes in the eternal game of laws and adds a new note to universal harmony, then man must have a reason, an intention or a goal. What goal? Scholars have never been able to discover one. They concluded that God is free, which means that man's crippled mind is incapable of understanding the animate intention. However, the difference between a free decision and an arbitrary one is small and infinitesimal. The real name of the God who creates this way is Chance.

The universe makes man just like it makes plants, animals, and the wind. Hence, there exists no conflict between what we call nature or Quetzalcoatl and us.

Artists have been able to give a visible, tangible, perfect, and perhaps unique form to this fact whose consequences disrupt all our philosophies (and it is probably for this reason that they chose to display this sculpture among so many other admirable ones).

Why is it perfect? Because the vision of man emerging from the mouth of the god is, one has to admit, monstrous. How can one tackle such a subject? The piece does not produce the expected effect at all. It is simply beautiful. This proves, without a doubt, that its creator was what one calls a genius, but also, I think, that the Unfathomable guided his hands.

Thus, in this sculpture, the impossible becomes beautiful. The impossible is that which the "ordinary" man, the ignorant man, the Greek who trusts his mind, takes to be impossible.

Yes, the American Indian is also ignorant: we all are, as long as we continue to believe that things are what the intellect shows them to be, that is, dualistic, and as long as we distinguish, for example, the body from the mind, appearance from essence, and the multiple from the one.

However, Mexican art, which is an ancient tradition, and peyote give to the American Indian the possibility to see that which is: a miracle.

For the dualistic mind, the supreme object of desire, unity, is always obtained by *the destruction of one of two opposing terms.* Hence, the Christian fights against evil and the flesh, this opaque and viscous thing inside him, which prevents him from blending with the good and the spiritual. Even Western philosophy wants to "remove the veil of appearance" in order to contemplate the essence. Also, following the example of alchemists, our scholars seek the secret of immortality: drugs to stop aging and ones that are capable of curing man of all his diseases.

From this dualism comes the determined and combative attitude that is so typical of the West. To the peyote enthusiast, this attitude seems pathetic because it inevitably generates mental strain comparable to the muscular strain and fatigue of the soul that we call anxiety, not to mention the thousands of dramatic, crazy, and unanswerable questions.

In order to see, all you have to do is put the intellect on the back burner. (This is what peyote does, even though the intellectual faculty remains intact.)

Consequently, I am no longer an alien on Earth. A convergence or a kind of osmotic exchange takes place. The barriers remain in place, but they are porous and translucent. Instead of turning their backs on me, things were revealing themselves.

As for the peyote enthusiast, he knows, sometimes with delight and sometimes with horror, his own *inhumanity.* He feels like a rock or a tree or a torrent; however, the man remains. (As we just said, the power to think and to distinguish good from evil subsists.) This is impossible, but it is so.

We can add that the main aim of art (and of genuine religion?) is to preach the doctrine of interpenetration. (I borrow this word from the Avatamsaka Sutra.) The sculpture I am talking about is an example in this sense. However, any piece of art worthy of this name combines these two seemingly contradictory elements, the *human* and the *inhuman,* in such a way that from their union is born the vision of the *superhuman,* of the being that is simultaneously man and stone, the vision of God.

The exhibition at the Petit Palais also taught me that Mexican civilization was not as "dark" as books have led us to believe.

The Western man who fears and *hates* death above all else, trembles with admiration in the face of this glorification of the remains and of the horror. Maybe he is secretly turned on by the mention of beautiful mangled flesh.

> *And all the bloody instruments of Destruction!*
> CHARLES BAUDELAIRE, *FLOWERS OF EVIL*

Not even for a minute does Western man doubt that another attitude is possible in the face of death. I once heard a pedant explain (to women, naturally) that the Aztec Earth goddess Coatlicue's hands reached out like grabbing claws and that her bare square teeth expressed eternal hunger.

However, the statue represented *a young woman,* albeit death, who was charming and "full of grace" and who was the feminine form corresponding to the Virgin Mary in Christianity. She took nothing and she received.

Thus, the simple black statue remained, as if invisible, in the worried crowd.

It said that death was always like springtime, new to everyone, sweet, flowery, and welcoming to all men. Like the Quetzalcoatl, this statue united and blended together what man dreads the most and that which awakens the most tender of thoughts.

Here again, the effort could have been and should have been colossal, but it was not. However, I had never suspected the fact that the Mexicans loved death like someone loves adolescence or the first day of spring; no book had ever allowed me to.

On the contrary, they had always, via dramatic theories, stressed the cruelty of it all, as if the words *human sacrifice* were enough to throw a dark veil over the true intentions of the works of art. However, it was obvious, to me at least, that the obsidian knife, the priest dressed in human skin and carrying a garland of orchids on his shoulders, and the altar flooded with blood and erect in the raging sky had an absolutely different meaning than the one our imagination credits them with.

I saw that the sacrifice was *natural*—inevitable, in a way.

It was what Christ's sacrifice no longer was; it probably had the same meaning at the beginning of Christianity, before hatred condensed into sects and deadly Paul mixed the fundaments of the church with hard Roman cement.

9

LOVE IS LIKE FIRE; FEAR IS LIKE ICE

Since Baudelaire's time the very possibility of verbal exchange has often been questioned seriously.

Indeed, nothing proves that I give words—the essential ones at least: *love, justice, God, freedom, salvation*—the same meaning as the person I am talking to does. The discussion normally leads to an agreement that is probably illusory. In the end, every word rests on an act of faith that today's skepticism, often all too legitimate, makes more and more difficult. We are no longer content to believe that we understand, and we prefer honest ignorance to misleading enlightenment.

Thus, even if we speak about everyday life, we have to protect ourselves from a feeling of helplessness and futility. Words seem cold and opaque. Is there a relationship between them and the dazzling heat that I am? A writer has no option but to ask this question. A membranous shadow hovers over his page.

No doubt the uncertainty fades away, and sometimes, for no

apparent reason, joy appears. Music reaches the depths of language, animates it, and lights it up, but these moments are brief. Generally, the writer just confronts his demons with an empty stubbornness whose value he is quick to deny.

Concerning the relationship that exists between events ("dimension") and feelings ("intensity"), rare are those who see its weakness.

A man's and woman's eyes meet: adding a comment seems unnecessary, at the least. Discretion, compulsory or almost, since Gustave Flaubert's time, differentiates Honoré de Balzac from the modern novelist.

Facts, as one would say, "speak for themselves," and pretty well. By listening to their language, one can guess the language of the heart, known to all. The gesture and the cry are enough: they are visible, audible, and objective expressions of emotions.

By only narrating what is actually happening—this strikes the indifferent observer—the author also gives a concise and dramatic turn to his narration. The process is effective and, in fact, so natural that no one notices it.

Thus, despite the prevailing skepticism, an understanding remains. It is a given that the *action* has the same meaning for everyone and plays the same tune on everyone's emotional keyboard. This salvages newspapers, books, and comedies. One can write and read and continue to believe that one is understood and that one understands. Doubt comes later, from Mallarmé or thinkers like Danish theologian and philosopher Søren Kierkegaard.

One could say that daily life is the ensemble of intelligible actions and that ordinary literature is the one that speaks about these actions.

This form of literature is, in a certain way, intentionally

superficial. For this reason, it is almost always indifferent to the writing style. Anxiety and depth originate from the writing style, as Flaubert has rightly proved.

He invented the process referred to here, but he used it in a different way altogether than his disciples do, except for German author Franz Kafka. Neither the events nor the feelings interested him. He wanted to *communicate.* This hope, or this obsession, makes him a poet.

That being said, the "map of facts" constitutes the basis, if one may say so, of the relationship that generally links the author to the reader. What is happening to me can happen to everybody; that is the axiom from which we draw the following corollaries: everybody can see what I see, and everybody can feel what I feel.

Then, and only then, one "casts a shadow" in order to show that things are not always as simple as we would like them to be, but the agreement is always considered as a given (with or without a ruse). Only a madman denies it, and for this very reason, excludes himself from society.

What happens when one uses an expander of the consciousness? I can see and feel *differently.* Thus, the description of the event is no longer enough. This event, minute indeed ("a bird flew by, a leaf fell to the ground"), echoes in the soul of the enthusiast with a force that seems exorbitant to the "profane." There is no longer a connection between the "dimension" and the "intensity." A distance is established that makes the reader *profane,* a humiliating word that, quite rightly, gives rise to indignation. What right does anyone have, he wonders, to adorn himself with the beautiful term *enlightened? Sick person* is a more suitable term. The writer does the best he can, so be it, and describes "the cloak of magnificence" (an expression inspired by the Sufi poet Ruzbihan Baqli), but this cloak is absolutely still, and no amount of wind can move its folds.

Thus, we have the simple and insurmountable obstacle: in the end, on a grand day, almost nothing happens from an objective point of view. An absolute silence of facts, a *disproportion,* which language cannot satisfy, appears, and it seems that this shows a new weakness of language. I am more alone than I was afraid of. I am brandishing the dark lamp of speech.

This is because, yet again, emotion in ordinary life is the daughter of action, and it is communicated provided the action has the necessary projection.

Nothing is like that in this case: gestures have a universality, a banality even, of the seasons; the comments are common or vague. (We shut them up for this reason.) Only the enthusiast is affected by his "adventures"; the fluctuations in his sensitivity seem strange and distant, like those of an animal or a madman, and they arouse cold and "scientific" curiosity. The magic blood, which determines the value of all exchanges, does not circulate between him and other men.

These observations explain and, I believe, justify the "subterfuge" I use in the pages that follow.

In chapter 10, "The Priest and the Vampire," I try to build a bridge between the inside and the outside in such a way that the reader can, to a certain extent, understand the enthusiast's feelings and, I dare not to say, share them.

Indeed, things happen that throw the story's main character into a state of confusion similar to the one provoked by the initial infiltrations of the cactus. I give the *plot* the role of peyote.

This plot naturally has a meaning (as the names Emmanuel and

Sophie indicate). To understand, one does not necessarily need to know that the author is thinking of peyote. A man is placed in certain circumstances that force him to question his life, his calling, his faith; let us go further and say the West and the God of the West.

Thus, these circumstances have exactly the same effect as the cactus does; as we have observed, by dilating the investigator's faculties, they reveal the limits of common perception to him, and as a result, they reveal the misery of the philosophies founded on this perception.

Having said that, I must admit to taking advantage of the "situation" for describing once again and from a different point of view the "dark period," as it is called: the meeting with the guardian or the dragon of the threshold, doubt and fall, agony and ecstasy. My story is fantastical only in appearance. In the end, things really do happen this way, even though the observer only sees a big man who is suffering and who no longer knows how to speak. (Oddly enough, we find the sentence, "I can't speak anymore," twice or thrice in Rimbaud's "A Season in Hell.")

Thus, we have a story—a good one or a bad one—in which the transition from violence to the light takes place without the slightest allusion to peyote. In fact it is an *image* true to the description, as far as possible, of a crisis that took place in New York in February 1960.

However, if most writers of prose describe events giving rise to emotions or thoughts and actions through which emotions manifest themselves more than the emotions themselves, it is not only because everyone knows love, fear, hatred, and so forth. It is also because the fluctuations of subjectivity are *undetectable,* in a certain way.

One can name them. One can also apply adjectives to them:

feelings are intense or weak, soft or painful. However—funny story—one cannot go further without resorting to images and comparisons that are all, or almost all, borrowed from the world of the senses.

So we declare that love is "like fire" or that fear is "like ice."

The thing is that vocabulary assigned to the expression of feelings is simultaneously poor and full of gaps. We lack the words that are necessary to describe with precision what we are feeling. We can say a million things about a chair: that it is small or big, strong or weak, beautiful or ugly. This has almost nothing to do with our feelings and emotions.

We talk about them all the same, no doubt, but because we are obliged to resort to images and comparisons to express ourselves, we abandon the map of prose and pure information.

When I say that love is "like fire," I am only doing what Baudelaire did in "The Balcony," for example, except that my expression is vague and common, whereas Baudelaire's is brilliantly accurate.

This obviously does not mean that I regard the faithful expression of feelings to be the only or even the main purpose of poetry. I simply want to point out the peculiarity of language (peculiarity, which is probably the root cause of the distinction that we make between the objective and the subjective).

I do not mean the same thing about a feeling than I do about an apple when I qualify it as red. In order to speak about a feeling, I must invent and imagine. I must introduce elements in my speech that, in the end, do not concern my actual words, in such a way that sometimes the reader cannot understand what I am talking about at all. (One can remember that Flaubert claimed that he only wanted to give the impression of the color yellow in *Salammbô*.)

Universality is the problem—and the salvation—of the poet. Love, death, God, freedom . . . The tremendous simplicity of the book of Genesis invisibly supports modern speech. The poet expresses the same thing as his precursors did, in a different manner. We know this and feel it, even when we hesitate, captivated by Daedalean charms, to name the theme of the work.

Calm block here fallen from obscure disaster . . .
"THE TOMB OF EDGAR POE," STÉPHANE MALLARMÉ

So be it, but this music is like the transcript of the unknown that we hold and that we are. I do not understand it, but I do not understand myself either, and this voice, which seems to rise from a torrent more than from a man, is infinitely human.

Surrealism does not mean unrealism, no matter what some people think. In this case, *sur-* signifies "super." If the philosopher speaks of essence and drives away the mystic from the place that is his homeland, then the mystic takes up residence in "the brilliant darkness of hidden silence"* and speaks about "suressence." Thus, the poet does the same thing; he wants to be more than realistic or surrealistic because the right word has been defiled.

In chapter 11, I try to express as precisely as possible the sensations of the enthusiast.

The apparent theme of the poem: a land of grandeur or desolation is born, as we have noticed, from the shortcomings of vocabulary. It is true that sometimes I have seen this land in my visions, sideways, and like one remembers. (An admirable page from Baudelaire's "Ruin (La Destruction)" allows one to think

---

*[From *The Doctrine of Infinite Growth* by Dionysius the Areopagite. —*Ed.*]

that opium and hashish lead their enthusiasts to these far-flung musings.)

However, the real subject of the text is something else. I wanted to—how can I put it?—make the sound of peyote audible, and that sound would be the same one that a *motionless breeze* would make. . . .

10

THE PRIEST AND THE VAMPIRE

One March day, as Father Emmanuel walked across the Pont des Arts, he noticed the willow tree of La Cité covered with its first leaves.

He stood there, motionless and in silence, for a moment, which seemed neither long nor short. The black and gray of the sky, the gray and black of the water, and the willow tree—the "angel of the willow tree," as he would call it later—seemed to be blowing in the wind. The priest heard the murmur of the city once again. He continued on his way.

The responsibilities of priesthood rarely allowed him to leave Paris, but that summer, he had the opportunity to spend a month in the country, at an old friend's place.

Mr. Joseph Nabre (that was the name of this friend) was crippled. Since the accident, which had ruined his career and killed his wife, he walked with difficulty, using two canes. He lived with his daughter in a white stone house surrounded by trees.

In his letter, Mr. Nabre spoke of his worries concerning Sophie's "strange and wild mood." The priest believed that his friend suffered mainly because he felt that Sophie was drifting away. The silences and the cold moments Mr. Nabre complained about led the priest to believe that there was a deeper problem, no doubt, but this problem, he believed, was the same one that every teenager suffered from.

However, when Father Emmanuel saw her waiting for him by Mr. Nabre's side on the railway platform, he knew that this explanation was too easy. Her face was still the one of the lively and frail child he had loved not long ago. However, the face now seemed poised on another one, like a mask; only the eyes were visible, and they were like green stones.

Other clues appeared the very same evening. Under the lamp, Sophie's forehead, neck, and hands seemed as if they were modeled in wax. Only the slightest hint of a tan veiled her paleness. Her hollow cheeks, the yellowish brown line highlighting her eyelid, and her colorless lips appeared like signs of suffering.

It was about midnight when the priest went back to his room. The room, with its whitewashed walls, low ceiling, and sunken floor, was quite big. The only ornament, in addition to the Christ in ivory hanging above the head of the bed, was an old mirror in an elaborate frame, whose darkened silvering, dotted with spots, reflected a dark and distant image. The priest hung his clothes in the closet. He pushed down the slats on the shutter and turned off the lights. Night came in.

Seated on the windowsill, he saw a kind of transparency invade the darkness little by little, and the big ghosts at the far end of the garden became trees again, while the sky behind them expanded.

In the hall downstairs, the clock struck once. He waited for the other strokes, but they did not come. The spell was broken.

Confused and sketchy memories flooded in now. Father Emmanuel was just a man, lost in thought.

He said to himself, "If I can only find trivial words to express what I am feeling, it is because these words are right. I can see trees, the sky, and a few stars; I can hear the insects and the stirring of the leaves when a breeze blows, and before this sight, I can feel . . ." He would have liked to say "God's presence," but he did not dare to.

This is what he was thinking about when an incident took place. Sophie's room was opposite his. He heard the latch creak. A few minutes later, a dark form crossed the garden and pushed the gate open. The priest strained to listen despite himself. The sound of the leaves muffled the sound of words being exchanged, without drowning out the sound completely.

Father Emmanuel would go to the village every morning to attend church service. He would return in time for breakfast. Mr. Nabre would wait for him on the terrace, seated in a large wicker chair with the newspaper on his knees.

Sophie would come and go, barefoot. The two friends would talk and sometimes play a game of chess. Then, as the day got hotter, Mr. Nabre would retire to his room. The priest would write letters, read his prayer book in the garden, or go for a walk.

A dirt road led to walls covered with wild flowers, and the bees gathered nectar from them with their powdery, jet-black heads. The priest liked to come to these ruins that people called "the hamlet," as if the name would suffice to make the scattered stones and worm-eaten beams a suitable place for man to live. The chapel, however, was intact. It was an oblong building with a porch held together by small pillars and a tile roof. The windows were boarded. It was far away from the hamlet in a grassy enclosure. Father Emmanuel had found a shady spot in a thicket among the tombs and the trees, which sheltered him from people's curious gazes.

Then, the land rose and was covered with bare and twisted oak trees. Having climbed up the slope, one reached a plateau where farm machines were moving their antennae to and fro.

Life was peaceful, but only on the surface. Every night, Sophie would slip out of the house, and the priest knew this. Sometimes, she would not return until dawn.

Even though she avoided him, he often had a chance to see her, observe her, and talk to her, and as the days went by, the young girl's strangeness confirmed some particular ideas.

She was pale under her tan and spent hours in the garden, inert, as if she were dead. The rest of the time, she was curt, tense, and bitter, but a wild light shot through her eyes.

Uneasiness filled the house. At noon, when the air was heavy like oil, the priest would feel dread come over him at the sight of a curtain rising as he walked across the hall. The cloth, bulging like a breast, played in the sun. Its shadow drew a tawny line, which curved and became blurred on the floor, but the priest did not see this graceful dance, or rather, this was not what he had seen. It was as if the very breeze, the innocent breeze, was conniving with the force that imprinted the curtain with this curve.

Images interfered with Father Emmanuel's nights. He tried to sleep, but the effort only gave rise to more dangerous images. There were bubbles, clusters of bubbles in a murky place, shivers running through them. Sometimes a bubble would burst with the soft and low sound of laughter. *One* knew what to expect. *One* was in the know. The priest felt the weight of a gaze that was immensely old and immensely disillusioned. A pulse emanated from his pillow, and he caressed and fondled every part of his body.

The only option was to go out and take a walk, but outside, danger adopted an even more sinuous way to get to the priest. Specks of dust hung in the sky and swelled with arachnid slowness. Some specks shone beyond them, surrounded by iridescent circles, and their sparkle became more and more intense, and their numbers increased.

Father Emmanuel was fascinated. Soon he would lie down and forget the insidious freshness of the grass, as well as the plots and hunting that went on beneath him. He became the earth, and that was not enough; he became stone, and the waves from the depths of the earth went through him. In the continuously expanding sky, these waves would cross others, which came from the invisible and which emanated from the powers.

"They do not *believe.*"

These words were spoken so softly and came from a mouth so near that Father Emmanuel thought he himself had said them, as if, while his soul was glorifying God, his mind had turned toward men.

However, it was another voice. It came from the street. The priest remained motionless, felt dizzy, and had a feeling that the voice was his all the same, but it was separated from him; it was floating in the air, charged with black specks, like a spirit.

"They don't even know what that means anymore," the voice said. "You always think about what would happen if the secret was discovered. It can never be discovered, and this is what you must understand. They have already decided that these are lies and that the . . ." One would have thought that a hand closed over the speaking mouth.

"Do not use that word, I beg of you. You know it horrifies me." It was a feminine voice.

"And that the . . . people of my kind do not exist. In such a way that danger does not exist either. I would like to see your priest at work. He is no more capable of hurting me with his Latin and his holy water than he is of consecrating his hosts. What lacks is force; what lacks is faith."

"My love," said the other voice. "My dearest love." It was Sophie's voice.

Father Emmanuel stood up.

"Please forgive me, Sophie. I laid down there. I do not want you to think that . . ." Sophie was alone. Despite the darkness, her face seemed very white. Her hand was placed on her throat, and this hand also seemed very white.

"It's you, Father," she murmured. "It's you."

"I startled you. I was asleep. I was having the strangest dream . . . the strangest dream."

She did not respond. She stayed still in the same position, her hand on her throat. Her forehead, her cheeks, and the bridge of her nose seemed carved in ivory. There was a gap between the priest and her and around them a million rustles and a million murmurs.

It was only the following day that the truth, or at least a part of the truth, appeared. He was seated in his room, at the window, watching the play of sunlight in the leaves. That is where the dreams formed. The priest saw a white disc, he saw fingers, and he saw his fingers holding a white disc. *Hoc est enim corpus meum.* He stood up, threw his book on the bed, ran a nervous hand over his face and through his hair. The book slipped off the quilt and landed on the floor with a dead thump.

By the time he overcame the dizziness, he was in the garden. The shock had been so violent at the time that he had fled like an animal. *What lacks is force; what lacks is faith.* His gaze turned toward the flowers, the hedges, and the grass where the smooth and secret roots of big trees crawled. The shadow was green and moved slowly, like water, around the bright islands made by the sunlight. Yes, this was it, this was it: the Crucified. . . . Laughter rose to the priest's lips.

Someone had boarded the windows and blocked the door with a chair. The chair was broken, and the boards were gray and cracked. Thick and heavy ivy glistening like mesh covered the small beams supporting the porch.

A big dragonfly flew by. With its spectral wings and bulky thorax, which led to an abdomen that was thin and slightly curved like a fiddlestick and inlaid with green and blue, and with its oval and lunar eyes, it seemed to belong neither to the day nor to the night. Its flight, which was sometimes fast and sometimes slow and punctuated with unexpected pauses and sudden intervals, recalled the impulses, halts, and volte-faces of the mind. My mind, Father Emmanuel said to himself.

The cemetery's dimensions seemed to disappear. In a more confined space, the tombs, bushes, and trees, cramped together, seemed like big balls of wool. The chapel shrunk. Slanting and sharp arabesques, like black glints, appeared.

Father Emmanuel stretched his numb legs. He was alive, and that was enough. Now, between him and those for whom this was not enough, a gap opened, which no words could fill. He pulled out his watch. The darkness multiplied the flickering lines on the dial and superimposed zigzags and bright stains on his hands.

The moon was rising. The chapel had the vaguely translucent aspect of a block of ice. "The chapel is dead," Father Emmanuel said to himself. However, the Earth was alive, the sky was alive; he could hear the insects in the grass, in the bushes, and in the stones, and in the distance the untiring and abstract fury of the dogs. Suddenly, he saw a white face under the porch.

A man stepped out of the darkness and came forward into the light. Then a woman came out of the darkness. Flower stalks and feathers clung to the bottom of her dress. The man slowly turned his head.

He was very tall and very strong. His curly hair had metallic tints. It came down on his forehead to form a tip, which emphasized the raised arch of his eyebrow. The bridge of his nose was hardly visible, in such a way that the nostrils, joined to the mouth by the line of the upper lip, seemed to belong to the bottom of the face. Sometimes, a greenish gleam, resembling a flame seen through water, appeared in his eye.

"One would say that I frighten you." It was the voice from the other night.

"You have changed so much. Changed so much."

He slowly moved his hand over his face, like one touches an unknown object. It was a big hand with thick nails.

"A beautiful tiger head." He stretched out his arm in the moonlight. "A beautiful tiger paw as well." In the distance an owl hooted. "I am united with the Earth; I am a force of the Earth. In the end, the body will undoubtedly mold itself into the form of the soul, won't it? That will be *good*."

"But I do not know who you are anymore!"

"When you will be like me, you will understand me, but for now, you cannot understand me, and I cannot understand you either. You want something, and you do not want it. I do not understand this. Me, I want something, and I do what I want to do. As for you, you are like the others."

He turned his face to the moon again.

"Every night, my strength grows. Every night, I become capable of new forms, and of course, it is true that I always have more trouble finding my own form. Soon, I will no longer return to it, and I will no longer want it. It is necessary to let this body go bad. I take the form of this body for you, because I can still remember who you are, but memory erases itself. In a little while, all of the past will be swallowed up."

"You told me that we would never change."

"It was because I did not know. I thought that you all would end up finding the body and destroying it. Now I know that it was *they* who abandoned it."

"But I do not want to die!"

"Die? Who is talking about dying?"

He seemed to be on a roll. Sophie spread her arms and stepped back, unsteadily, as if she had been hit. The wind rustled through the treetops.

Once again, it was like the other night. The branches cracked, the leaves swayed; the breeze in the grass and the scurrying of the mice, all the noises that filled the fields composed a noisy map instead of melting away into each other, like a place with currents, banks, islands, and gulfs of silence.

Father Emmanuel raised his head. Widespread wings glided high up in the sky, and the priest liked the cold and the wind. Then the circle of his flight closed in, and the bird looked down and saw a face flooded with tears, hovered around it some more, and landed delicately. It was a force that was neither good nor bad; the priest said to himself, "Force."

The man took Sophie in his arms, held her close to him, and bent forward. A blaze descended on the couple and enveloped them both. This blaze rolled and gleamed. Its inclined crest growled and shone under the force of the wind. Another, narrower blaze joined the bigger one, mixed with it, and melted into it. The two strident blazes rose up together into a spiral.

That was when Father Emmanuel stood up. He separated the bushes and walked toward the chapel.

The man stepped forward. His strange eyes expressed neither surprise nor anger. They only stared at the approaching stranger dressed in black. Sophie was lying in the grass. She was between the priest and the man, and behind the man, a million stars trembled.

"Father, Father," murmured the man, "you can do nothing to me. Why are you provoking me?" Was he talking? No, a voice said to Father Emmanuel; the other man's lips had not moved.

The priest stepped over Sophie's body. The words he wanted to say stuck in his throat, yet the other man understood.

"How cold you must be. Ah, it's fear. I had forgotten about fear. You are afraid, yet you want to know something. I cannot understand this. . . . Yes. But I only know what I am. And I am . . ." A dark frown changed his face. It was as if something from afar had touched him. "You were with me, up there. You knew my joy. I could feel you. I am . . . Your question is crazy. I do not understand it any more than you understand me."

"But you were a man!" the priest shouted.

"Fool."

Father Emmanuel stood up and separated the bushes. "Fool." He walked toward the chapel. Who had said that word? He could still hear it resounding in another barred space. He rubbed his sore shoulder. One side of his cassock was covered with mud. "Fool."

From time to time, big, dark wings fluttered over the church's facade. Clouds glided past the moon; it was their shadow. No one was there. Father Emmanuel left the cemetery. The earth on the path formed bumps and holes under his feet, causing him to stumble along his way.

The light shining through a window reflected a long, gray rectangle in the grass, in which a black cross was inscribed. Father Emmanuel crossed the garden and entered the house. Mr. Nabre was in a dressing gown; his fingers clenched his walking stick. The robe's open collar revealed his chest hair.

"Emmanuel! What happened to you? It's been hours. . . ."

The priest sat down. He absentmindedly began to scratch at the dry earth on his cassock and remove the seeds and twigs that clung to it. Moths fluttered around the lamp.

"I lost my God." These words were uttered as if by someone else. Now it was too late; everything would come out. A fog thickened. He once again heard the moths bang against the lampshade and the ticktock of the clock. Mr. Nabre seemed bigger and heavier. His features were dark. The silence continued.

"Look." He pointed to an area on the wall with his walking stick. The paint had formed a kind of bump there. The light played on the ruggedness, forming a face. "And there." The stick pointed to another area. "And there is also this one and that one." As the stick moved, one could have said that the wall was coming to life. There were lips, crushed foreheads, protruding chins, teeth, and eyes full of hatred and irony. The wall was becoming a veil through which one could distinguish another place. The place was alive; it pulsed and swarmed, and the heads invaded the ceiling and the floor slats. Father Emmanuel looked toward the window. A huge, leafy face was pressed up against the windowpane.

"I did not tell you everything," said Mr. Nabre. "I myself also thought that it was madness." He corrected himself. "It *is* madness, but that changes nothing."

"She goes out every night," said the priest.

"I know."

"She meets a man."

"A man?" His voice traveled to the darkest corners of the house. "Are you a man?"

The priest's hands were sweaty. Mr. Nabre turned away heavily. He picked up a bottle on the table and poured a brown liquid into his glass. Then he added some water. The dark circles that covered his cheeks, the point of his polished red nose, the folds in his skin, and the bluish nerves on his temples revealed his old age in a way that was almost unbearable. A devious gleam slowly appeared in his eyes.

"Be careful," he murmured. "Be careful." His hand was trembling slightly. He put the glass down.

"I am afraid," Father Emmanuel said.

"*We* are afraid," Mr. Nabre softly said.

The ceiling was lower, and the closet was bigger and blacker. He picked up the book; his fingers stuck to the pages. The pages were covered with ants. They did not move; they were dead. Bright wires hung out of a gaping hole in the ceiling. The walls bent forward, and the floor was giving way. He could no longer remember. His head was filled with thick darkness. The old names were there, on the other side. He could not reach them.

He was still holding on to the book. Slowly and painfully, he deciphered the letters. The hand holding the book was big with thick nails.

He was seated on the ledge of the window. Shadows ran along on what remained of the road. He understood; once again an unending stream of water flooded the street. He put the book down and stood up. He no longer knew how to read, but he knew that it was a book.

His gaze moved over milky spaces full of hideous heads. Extreme caution was now necessary. He approached the mirror. Eyes with watery circles hovered in the brown air of the other room. The room was empty.

Shadows trembled on the road. The road was white. He stopped. Night was rustling in the fields, and the fields were gushing like water running down a slope. He saw the image of Mr. Nabre slumped in a chair with a wound on his throat.

He pushed the image away. He had to. Did he have to? That was the worst thing of all. There were mouths, thousands of them. They were laughing. There were slits in the stones and cracks in the trees. The grass chuckled, and thousands of black, pointy tongues licked thousands of black, wet lips.

The time had come. He was now following a dirt road. The names disappeared one after another like extinguished lamps. A yellow ball was on the horizon. It puckered up and subsided. Brown lines cut into it. They thickened and frayed. A wall came up, like a thorny fence.

"You are one of us now," the man said. He was leaning against the wall. His lips were immobile. Sophie was at his side. She had tall, membranous wings, and her eyes shone with an electric, green gleam.

"Did I kill him?"

The man did not answer. His arms were crossed. Sophie unfurled one wing, then the other. She had traces of blood on her chin and her cheeks.

"Shall we go? It will be dawn soon."

"This is impossible. Sophie . . ."

The man placed a big hand on Father Emmanuel's chest.

"She is mine. Do not touch her."

The priest stepped forward. It was as if he were walking into a wall. Then the man's hand entered his chest. He took another step. The big teeth were very close to his face. He took a third step. A paleness rose from the ground. Sophie collapsed against Father Emmanuel like a stone.

The easiest words. He had come. He had come at night by the paths of the night. He had come in a black robe, in silence. The robe stifled him; it was too tight at the neck, and it stuck to his skin like the fire of death. He could not take it off. He was the black man, and he was stifling Sophie is his black arms, and the easiest words were still lacking. She was trembling.

"The truth," the priest said. "The truth." His voice broke. "Everywhere I go, there is darkness. You cannot stay with me."

She raised her forehead. Her eyelids were shut. She was listening to another voice. Dawn colored the childish arch of her lip. Suddenly her gaze shone.

"The willow tree. Do you remember the willow tree?"

Who had spoken? He was thrown to the floor, his head banged against the stones, and his fingers swept through the dust. Sophie's hair fell on his face, and her shiny, red face was bent over his. She was on top of him, crushing him into the ground. An immense weight crushed him.

"It was . . . death. . . ."

"You gave it another name."

Light filled the priest's head. White, dazzling, and deadly, it rolled in from the depths of the universe, toward him, wave after wave.

"I am here," Sophie said. He groped, blindly. His fingers met a smooth shoulder, a neck, and a mouth.

"The angel . . . The angel of the willow tree . . . It is you."

"They are waiting for an explanation," Father Emmanuel said.

Sophie brought the priest's hand to her lips. The road was noisy and blue; the horizon shone. In the valleys, a lazy mist rose.

"I was walking with you," Father Emmanuel said. "I will tell them that. I will also tell them that dawn came."

"One only talks to men at night."

"Do not mock men," Father Emmanuel said. "They were with us during the night. Your father was with us. I told him everything. He, too, was afraid. He told me so. We carried our fear together."

"But it is you who came out; it is you who came."

The priest did not answer. They were getting closer. The leaves behind the gate were moving, and blue stains moved on the sunny ground. Mr. Nabre was on the terrace, and he was waiting; he was waiting for them.

"Give up," Sophie said. "Give up once and for all. It is bad pity that is troubling you. It clouds your words. You must be absolutely simple; say what is. This is the secret of patience." She bent down and picked up a stone. The priest took it, felt its weight, and ran his finger over its lines, over its scorched cracks. "They want to know how you see him," Sophie said, "but they do not want to see him."

"I was holding on," Father Emmanuel said, "to memories, if you like. I was a man under my black robe; I wanted to be that man and, if the robe tore, continue to be a man. It is like calling a spade a spade, a table, a chair, and a lamp. I could no longer do it, but I was holding on. I told myself that it was a matter of time. I had to go on. One minute more, one second more. I told myself that if

I really could not go on, there was death. Then I understood that death would solve nothing. It was absurd to continue to be a man if the man had invented the names. This is what torments them and tempts them, of course. Be like the sea; be like the wind! Why not? I would have those crazy eyes that cause cold shivers."

"It is time," Sophie said. She pressed up against him and wrapped her arms around him. "It is time."

"So," the priest said, "I gave in. Light came in. You were speaking about the willow tree, and I saw that we were in it, you and me. There was no silence."

She moved away. Her breast rose. She pushed the gate open. Then she turned around and stretched out her hand. The priest took it.

"Come," she said. They entered the garden.

11

IMHOTEP

A black, shapeless mass.

A man was sleeping in the room, and there was a black, shapeless mass in this man's head. I looked at him. The man was me, but what was the right name for this black mass in the mental pocket moving slowly under my gaze?

I was not asleep. Immobile and attentive, I maintained a distance.

Sometimes a piece of darkness collided with another, and a deathly, pale needle would fall from it. You could call it a ghostly spark.

Rapidly moving faces circulated under this uncertain light.

The faces looked like whips. They crisscrossed with shivers and jolts. Crossing each other, they drew riblike forms; the tips of these ribs would stretch out, twisted and disheveled.

I could distinguish one reddish bulk from the other in the cracks. Their rounded surfaces glowed feebly. They looked like skulls. They had jagged edges, as if they were imitating the sutures of skulls, but they had neither the rigidity of bone nor its stillness.

They were like whips with shivers running through them.

They would swell up, multiply, and invade the empty space that I was struggling to maintain between us. They struggled to make up the distance as much as I struggled to maintain it. My effort gave them the energy needed for the proliferation.

It thus became necessary to stop, to accept the possible suffocation of the consciousness by the unknown, all in all, to defeat fear. This would determine a decisive change.

The withered bulks began to melt; the darkness absorbed them little by little and swallowed them up. Then the thinning whips disappeared. There was a burst of light.

I could explore the stratifications of time on the condition that I stayed in contact with the Earth.

My explorations always had the same destination. A changing route would bring me to a deserted land of another age. I felt like it was here alone that I could know true bliss. Upon returning, I would vainly search for an explanation about this conviction. I had always lived in a temperate climate. Where was the longing for the desert coming from?

A string of salt lakes showed that this region had once belonged to the sea.

These lakes were huge but not very deep; they were connected to each other by narrow, sandy streams. Some of them, not having the basaltic bedrock that assured their neighbors of a waterproof finish, had dried up. Only a white expanse remained, and a steep slope determined their limits.

Other lakes were surrounded and even covered with reeds that relentlessly swayed in the wind, banging together like slats of cardboard, an endless battle of specters mixed together with the crumpling of silk.

Sometimes the sound would get louder, become a sigh, a sob, or a call.

Tall cacti in the shape of candelabra marked the approach to the desert. They stood at the entrance to the desert like statues of the gods.

I indeed felt as if I were flying above some colossal temple.

Huge, rocky structures arose at what seemed to be regular intervals. Beheaded mountains presented cracks and rippling ridges in their upright sides, and the whirling debris spread out on all sides as far as the eye could see, to finally fade away into the prismatic horizon.

The sight of all this desolation created a peculiar shock, the inexplicable conviction that I was seeing the land of my childhood once again.

I was not wrong: there exists a childhood of the soul just like a childhood of the flesh; the soul takes shape like the seed takes root. It was here that I had joined myself to the Earth for the first time, by this tangible offshoot, the human foot.

The wind that disheveled the dunes had once filled my nostrils. I had seen the sun retrieving its long, red rays and disappearing behind the hills, one by one, like a spider goes into its hole. I had looked for the black, iron tears that fall from the stars in the sand; as my fingers touched them, my imagination would go to the top of the willow trees that I had given beautiful names.

What disturbed me the most was perhaps the way time passed by. The mind would measure time according to the wind, the rocks, and the sand. According to the mind, a second occupied as much time as a century on the dial of a sidereal clock. A second and a century refracted the prodigious light of the great universal diamond with equal accuracy.

However, within me, the consciousness of the temporary superimposed itself on the consciousness of the eternal.

I could not forget my other body lying in the dark room, and each minute brought its disappearance nearer.

The desert was less peaceful than I initially thought it was. A kind of impatience and nervousness was perceptible. Sometimes the low wind sifted through the sand and knocked over the reed as if it were looking for something. Then it thrust toward the horizon, banged into a dark obstacle, and turned away. There was a continuous growth of agitation beneath things.

The agitation was contagious. I myself was bumping into the limits of the unlimited. I was hoping for impossible release. Despite myself, I participated in waiting for the unknown.

However, who was waiting? Who was awaited? Who was suffering? Who had the power to end this spreading pain?

No face showed itself, but I could feel a presence everywhere.

There was neither a mouth to speak from nor ears to listen through, but there was a deep, silent plea and some reverberation or another where the possibility of an answer formed, confusedly, in the infinite.

The sensation intensified when I looked at the sky. A form began to take shape there, a rough shape that was constantly erased and then drawn again. It could be seen through the clouds.

One could see several cores linked together by threads.

Steam rolled out from the blowing wind around this skeleton-like form.

It formed a saurian jaw, an oblong skull, which stretched out into the toothed waves of the vertebrae, skinny arms and huge hands spreading out their crystalline phalanges in the milky stratifications of the atmosphere.

Even though this being was mixed with the clouds, it did not mistake itself to be the clouds. The being would shine with immense, ecstatic pain. I allowed words, always the same words, to express the unlimited joy and the insatiable desire: "Ah, to live," the being seemed to sigh, "to live, to li–i–ve . . ."

The being was gigantic, fragile, terrible, and pathetic all at once. It would passively suffer the decomposition of the clouds. It had no memories of its previous existence and no feeling toward its future existence. It was confused with the perpetual change of the present. It was like consciousness in its protoplasmic state.

I was reaching the end of the desert. A black line held back the diffusion of perspectives, and this line got thicker and wrinkled up. A cliff formed, like a curtain on the horizon, and spread a stony drape on the ground. After going around the cliff I entered a beautiful, green valley.

Big trees grew in the valley.

As I got closer, I saw a large brown surface, which moved in a serpentlike way, between the trunks: it was a river.

A fabulous sight awaited me on the other side: I saw a temple, the same temple whose remains I thought I had seen in the desert.

It was not a rough guess; it was the temple. I recognized it immediately.

I saw that the pile of rocks, which I had mistaken for ruins, were, in fact, beams and that the debris was, in fact, the incomplete construction of a project that was slowly coming out of the chaos and meeting the supreme outline of reality here.

The gods lived in the temple. Some of them were standing up, as if they were about to walk; others were sitting down with their backs straight, their legs folded, one hand closed, and the other spread out on one thigh. The setting sun threw its golden light on their squashed faces, and the night that followed spread its huge, black traits all the way down to their feet.

No one was there. The men who had built this temple and given the gods their faces and names were dead. Did it matter? The inhabitants of this temple did not need worshippers. They were grand. They were the Ancient Beings, the Powerful, the Masters, the Fashioners, the Victorious, and the Destroyers. They wore the crown, they held the scepter, and they knew the rules. Man, the docile tool, had accomplished his task, and then he had disappeared. Everything was all right.

Nevertheless, the intruder had been spotted. He was watched. The gods watched him.

They showed no malice. Malice, like benevolence, was just an emotion, and they paid no heed to emotions. They may have seemed to be in favor of those who respected the rules and hostile to those who broke them, but they were neither hostile nor favorable; they were, in the face of man's noise, the ambassadors of the original silence.

They were looking at me. They were looking at the snake crawling up the wall of the temple, the river, the trees, the purple bracken in the hollow of the cliffs in the evening light, and the black and shifty bracken formed by the movement of the breeze in the clouds; the first stars appeared in the rising mist, looking like pink stains, and they formed bright cracks in the window of the sky as the mist spread. They were watching, and they did not speak.

The silence ended.

It was hardly any louder than the vibration of blood in my ears. Like this vibration, it was a compact, persistent, and continuous sound something like the growl of a waterfall reduced to a murmur because of the distance.

Unformed words burst forth.

It was the confused sound of a voice. There was the sound of a faraway torrent and the whispering sound of a voice nearby. One could understand, one thought that one could understand, and then one heard only the hammering of the water on the rocks.

There were intervals in the hammering; at times it became inaudible, as if erased by the rustling of the leaves of the neighboring riverbank.

The hammering became full and deep. Soon it would be too loud for other sounds to cover it up: now the hammering covered up all the other sounds. However, it maintained its ambivalent character; it was a torrent and a voice.

As a torrent, it would move from rock to rock, its wild arches and mane creating sparks like claws; as a voice, it would announce the eruption of dark forces into the real, which defied the core of the prophecy, ordered lightning on the holocaust, overturned the throne, and split the sea in two.

Suddenly, it became impossible to doubt: it was really a voice, and it resounded through the temple and the valley—a full, rounded, fierce, and sculptural voice.

"In the past, before men, we were!"

The past opened the door to the beginnings, but these beginnings were seen with an eye larger than the human one, and the consciousness that threw its colossal gaze on the jubilation of the elements felt no fear. On the contrary, it participated in the frenzy, united with it, and swam with the elements in bloody smoke, which formed at the surface of the chaos.

The "we" had the supreme height of certainty and brought the confused harmony of the vastness into the power of unity. The plural was singular, and the singular was an alliance of thunders.

However, the verb, briefly separated from the "we," was the supreme word.

It continued to hover over the "we" in a field without limits. It added the fear of vastness to the fear of heights.

"In the past, before men, we were!"

Yes, they were! The beauty of the affirmation destroyed all limits.

It spoke about the infinite expansion of the Substance in eternity.

The gods formed a new circle in the continuously expanding circle of the word; they floated in the glory of the Father like archipelagoes of glory.

I saw the agitation reach the profoundness.

The gods were returning to time, rolling once again in the mutations of the Effluvium, stretching out their muscles stiffened by centuries of immobility; they arched their backs and breathed out the purple air of slumber from their nostrils.

Fuzz now covered what used to be their smooth and polished skin; it covered their stomachs and chests, filled up the hollows and ledges, invaded their cheeks, and rooted into their foreheads. Then the fuzz became hair, the hair became a mane, and the mane rose up. Pale stains fell through the darkness, and I could see almost-liquid silhouettes there.

Their faces were really terrible. They had a claylike consistency, and their features crumbled under one another.

Their yellow lips formed points and butted out into a horn or spread out like a muzzle. An energy molded their hands and feet. Sometimes the nails would turn into claws; sometimes fingers that were stunted and welded together condensed into shoes.

Their fur became green and burgeoned. Their eyelids were swollen with resinous tears. Their shoes would split to become forks; they would fork out some more and thrust their woody swarms into the grass.

The leaves were already lending their ears to the secrets of the rain. The feminine abundance of their height brought out the purity of their stories.

Higher up, ink dispersed in sprawling puddles and formed octopus-like waves; the octopi grasped the debris; the debris broke apart in the murky wind.

Then the great descent began. The enormous formlessness crumbled. You could see the precipice collapsing, creating round heaps attached to one another by membranous lace the color of raw liver with the paleness of mushrooms, cataracts of melted lead, and fountains of sulfur molding the insides of the gargoyle's mouth; all the commotion of the downpour was breathing down the sinister porches and widening with every crazy bolt of lightning.

It was as if the vision had sucked me up. The other senses opened up to what the sight could not perceive, and, in turn, they poured into each other.

Light had a smell. Smells would fizz, buzz, twitter, and trill. There were tones of red iron and effusions of liquid bronze.

I was the sprouting force of the seed and a blue flame lined with crimson; I was the jubilation of the ferocious beast tearing at its prey and the arpeggio of terror in the torn prey.

Everything ended in the universal Effluvium.

The rain ran down my branches; I streamed with the rain in the branches, with the waves of the pebbles, with lava in the veins of the Earth, with blood in the veins of man, and with man in the veins of nations.

However, the being remained throughout the metamorphosis. A crystal-like element went on and continued. It was the same under scales as it was under skin; it was the same in the violence of the hurricane as it was in the silence of the gulfs. The man remained, and he knew it.

The man was me. I stayed connected to my native land by an essential root and by a very strong ligament to the navel of my origin.

For a fraction of a second, I believed that the ligament would give way. It did, as a matter of fact. I crossed the dark line and united my life to the unknown life.

The illusion lasted for a fraction of a second; this second was enough for the dream to interpose itself, a barely noticeable slipping that I wanted to stop, but it was too late. The very fact that I wanted to stop it quickened the movement. I no longer participated in the action of the gods; I thought I was participating in it. I no longer understood it, but I could remember having understood it. When did this happen? In the past, in time immemorial.

Not only did the faces of the dream separate me from fullness, they also denied its existence and unfurled the pure prospect of emptiness in the mind.

I looked at the furniture in my room with surprise.

This was a chair, that was a wardrobe, and the fluttering wings on the table were sheets of paper. In the mirror, the ghost whose eye sockets and nostrils were filled with blackish lichen was a reflection of me, blurred in the twilight. I knew this, no matter what. No, I no longer knew. Oblivion drew a pale circle in my head, going around a deadly, pale spot and slowly pushing away the ghastly wrinkle from its contour.

I ran my hand over my face, my neck, and my chest. The ghost in the mirror imitated me, and the pale stain of my shirt looked like a spider stretching out its long, black legs.

Where were the gods? They were still there. The transparent darkness swarmed with reefs and thick, still shadows. Darkness swarmed like water on their engulfed foreheads, and on the tips of their crowns, seaweed clung like stars.

I was in the desert again.

The desert always offered the dazzling aspect of fierce fixity.

However, I could feel a change rising up under the passive surface of the ground.

There was a shift in the constellations. New stars now shone their rays on the Earth.

The signs of tremendous fatigue showed up everywhere in the dazzling daylight.

The hills had the scaly, gray skin of extreme old age and a mood of despondency. Their skeleton was intact, but also more visible than it had been before. It grimly climbed up the bare, hilly landscape and the limestone sediments.

The deep cracks in the rock turned their reptilian openings toward the sky and drew thirsty, poisonous faces on the rock's surface.

The desert poured its sand into the valley through these cracks, forming long and wide slopes that spread out like a fan. Unusually stiff trees grew over there, and they hid their angular and hairy limbs under the superimposed patches of a thorny shell. Farther away, the grass bowed down in the wind.

The deterioration and aging could also be seen at the bottom of the valley.

The flow of water had hollowed out something like a muddy path and marked the riverbanks with its erosive work. Trees stood firmly along the path, and their roots descended deep into the water. The water spluttered and bubbled as it made its way through this network of knotty and twisted clumps, from which beards of foam hung.

A few fallen trees formed rotting heaps, and the waves around them widened their concentric circles, pouring out a yellowish cream like the ferments of stagnation.

The shadows lying in the folds of the earth had a purplish tint.

The sky had also changed. Thin and flat clouds bent over the horizon. They were still and formed veins of white marble in the blue sky. The wind blew beneath them.

I thought that the temple was intact, but its roof had crumbled. The daylight had ruined the solemn darkness of the rooms.

Stone poked through the cracks in the painting, like thick fog around the faces that one could still distinguish, grasping them with its red fingers, covering them, and taking hold of them. It insidiously ate away at the painting, starting at its very core, sometimes allowing a gesture, a smile, or an attitude to surface.

The obelisks showed their damaged facade in the daylight, and the grand statues of the gods lay broken among the colonnades.

Broken, they were even bigger than before. Their ruins were like the ruin of a world, and their fall shook the ground. The fall was the achievement of the impossible.

However, this achievement added a dimension to the universe. It denied the impossible. The gods returned to the darkness, just as they had come out of it. Their march was silent and prodigious; it ignored the difference between a dream and reality.

Their gnawed smile was fascinating. It was a sign, a hint, or a secret. Their giant heads, kissing the ground with leprous mouths, maintained an authority that was higher than earthly intelligence and that survived death's obliteration.

Lichen covered their eyes, but their greenish pupils never stopped seeing.

I rose higher.

The clouds were still far away, and they broke away in wisps, forming cameos against the deep blue sky. Down below, between the river bank and the bottom of the cliff, the temple was spread out like a pile of rubble.

I could see the layout of the rooms. I could distinguish the squares from the rectangles and the interlocked circles: geometry and dust. Big, dark numbers drawn on the floor indicated the silhouette of the walls and the columns: it was as if the sun, by outlining them with a golden line, confirmed their permanence, as if their fading was just an illusion and did not alter the substance of their affirmation in any way.

What struck me was the likeness of this sight and the one that the desert had presented before. It was the same sight. The area was overrun by the poison of the ruin and had led to its own destruction, uniting the crawling of the fissures, the oscillation of the loose stones, and the engraving of the erosion.

It had changed poison into ferment and misfortune into destiny. It had lived its own death.

The debris also represented a rough sketch like the desert. It was a preliminary sketch, an active thought, and a sincere intention to draw out the angles and proportions of the future temple from the ramifications of that which is possible. The end taking place before my eyes, caught up in the spiral of the wheel of time, was melting away into an unknown beginning.

"Our laws are dead!"

I recognized that voice. It had always been powerful, solemn, and sublime, but the echo made it sound weak and broken, as if it had come through an abyss. That was when I understood my mistake and why I could no longer feel the presence of the gods like a wonderful hand at the site.

Their gaze did not move under the lichen: it was another gaze, a new one, and little by little it modeled the pupil to resemble it.

They no longer inhabited the rest of their faces. A new name awaited the mouth capable of pronouncing it.

The gods, separated from death, were now separated from reality. They were ghosts that appeared to the ghost of a sleeping man, and they disappeared at dawn, like worms.

The wind was free. It wandered among the ruins into a shroud of sand whose folds trembled slightly as they crawled up the unconscious faces.

The stone was also free. Returned to the virginity of the origin, it awaited the faces of new masters.

The ancient masters were forever still. They did not participate in the perpetual polarization of terrestrial powers into the future. They were bound to the day when their faces had been uncovered; they inhabited the statue, as if frozen for centuries.

CONCLUSION

But the angels of the inmost heaven are naked.

EMANUEL SWEDENBORG

Peyote had given a goal to my existence. Before I took it, I had pretended to have one. Deep down, I did not know what I wanted. I was living in perpetual indecision. Only writing saved me from dissolution.

Now I can at least give a name to the object of my ambition. I know that I am looking for *illumination*. I want to become what Prince Siddhartha became under the Bodhi Tree.

In my opinion, this desire lies in all men, but most of them ignore it, obsessed with worries and futilities. They pursue the "wrong things," that is to say, things whose possession is incapable of giving them durable satisfaction.

As for the philosophers who look for or claim to look for knowledge, their judgment is clouded as well. Indeed, they confuse authentic knowledge with knowledge that can be obtained through the intervention of the mind. This is the worst illusion. Reason is earthbound; the spiritual and the divine elude him.

Thus, in a certain way, peyote separated me from men; the goals I aim for differ from theirs.

I no longer desire security or glory or fortune or power, not even knowledge, which is the same as security. (The intellect does not want to know at all; it wants to put an end to ontological bareness.)

However, I am also closer to men than I was before. I no longer differentiate their difficulties from my own, the obstacles between them, and their illumination from what I myself experience.

To put it in another way, I am no longer *alone*. It seems to me—quite inexplicably—that the efforts of others help me and that my efforts help others, that together, under a turbulent and dark sky, we are all looking for the place and the formula.

Peyote also changed my conception of the structure of the mind.

Certain elements of this structure, which had seemed insignificant until now, acquired extreme importance.

I do not know what Gurdjieff's cosmology is worth, but his horrible portrait of man seems right to me. Like him, I believe that all the ideas put forward by moralists and philosophers are based on an untruthful posit. They all presume that we are conscious, that is, free, yet, we are not. The ignorance of this fact distorts our thoughts and actions. We are like buckled wheels.

That being said, the exercises that I practiced had disappointing results. I am not any more lucid than I was before. Like Hugo would say, "Dreams, those clouds, interpose their folds and their transparencies over that star, the mind."

However, I became aware of my lack of consciousness in a certain way.

The memories of my grand days—memories full of nostalgia, I admit—allow me to compare and measure the gap between what I want to be, what I know I can be, and what I am.

Ghosts play between my gaze and the object in the form of

thousands of wandering and vain thoughts. How do I get rid of them? I do not know, but at least I ask the question, and sometimes for a few seconds it so happens that my sight becomes pure, and life takes on the tensile, crystalline quality of transparency.

In addition to this, I have become extremely sensitive to the lack of consciousness in other men.

This lack of consciousness is like a thin layer that I sometimes call the "patch."

It is as if they are wearing contact lenses without their knowing it, but they are wearing dark contact lenses that disturb and taint their perception instead of making it clearer.

To put it in a better way: it seems to me that all of them (almost all of them) are obsessed with imaginary worries that prevent them from fully participating in the movement of existence. If I may venture a simplistic comparison, they listen to heavenly music like one listens to a conversation when one has a migraine.

This is because their "little machine," like I sometimes call it, monopolizes the best part of their attention. They lend an eager ear to its rattling, granting sporadic and angry attention to the rest, to "what is," to quote the Indian writer and philosopher Jiddu Krishnamurti.

The relationships I establish with the vast majority of my contemporaries are difficult and illusory, thanks to the "little machine." They ask me to admire them, honor them, and even love them; they measure the affection that I have for them based on the respect with which I treat this absurd device. Thus, they force me to either shut up or lie. In my opinion, the "little machine" is a thing, a complicated toy whose agitated movement represents only a semblance of life.

Peyote deeply transformed the nature of my perception as well. The messages I receive from my senses are different from those I used to receive, like a colored photograph is different from a black-and-white one.

I am constantly conscious of my organism. The blue factory of thought pulses under a dead sky. The flowers of air sway in my nostrils. My mouth is like a shadowed beach. My lungs, like twin cathedrals, are full of bubbles that overlap, rise, thicken, melt into each other, squeal, and glisten faintly. The tropical zone starts further down, like a humid jungle where torrential monsters are on watch in the purple darkness.

A net of pain tightens around me. As soon as I am no longer absorbed in my work, I can feel the bones of my skull weigh on my mind, and the two snakes of the skillful caduceus run up my spine. Sometimes, when I lend an attentive ear to the immensely frightening murmur, I am seized by dizziness.

I see the Effluvium in everything, albeit less clearly than while under the influence of peyote. A force appears, and this force is beyond name, form, and objects, even though it manifests itself through them. It is like light, invisible, thanks to the screen on which it reflects.

I can say nothing about this force, or rather, I can only make small talk about it: this force is "life," "God." However, I know that others have seen it and know it: the sculptor Rodin, for example. From this force are born hips, as if from the sound of the sea, necks sculpted in loving heat, couples like serpentine bouquets, outflows, entwinements, and hair that are fountains, and these fountains are women, like an august and black feast of bronze.

The main change that peyote brought about is undoubtedly the following one: it transformed what I call the "me," for want of a better term. It is very difficult to talk about this change.

Language does indeed prevent us from correctly describing the relationship that an individual maintains with the world. If we rely on language—yet, we can think only if we rely on it— we are forced to believe that consciousness is the fundamental characteristic of the subject, the substance of the word *I*. As a result, the fundamental characteristic of the object can only be unconsciousness.

Seen in this light, what differentiates me above all from my body, for example, is the fact that I am aware of it, whereas my body is not aware of me at all.

This "obvious fact," at least since the time of Descartes (in fact, since Parmenides), is the basis of Western philosophy. It is the reason why we are *identified* to consciousness and thus to thought.

From this identification, dualism is born. To be more precise, this identification is dualism itself. If I believe that "being is thinking," I inevitably must also believe that what does not think is not. Therefore, the whole world is an illusion. (Be careful not to mistake this concept with the Eastern one of cosmic illusion.) Life appears, death appears, and "the marvelous clouds" appear, but the veil cannot be torn away, and it sticks to me like Nessus's shirt, burning and suffocating me. In fact, dualism transforms the world into a terrible film in which all the actors, except man, are machines, a point of view that is strangely similar to the one schizophrenics seem to have. . . .

Peyote freed me from my "me," in other words, from the image I had previously formed of the relationship I had with the world; I had been mistaken and blinded by language. It was an image that superposed itself on the real relationship and dissimulated it.

It is true that as long as I rely on language, I cannot, no matter how hard I try, see that God is in all things and that all things are in God. There was always a conscious subject on one hand and an unconscious object on the other, and between the two, an empty black space, which I vainly filled with questions. There was always a "me" (imperceptible to the rest) and "another" that the anguish demonized, so to speak.

Peyote dissolved opposition, but just like the masters who teach in silence, peyote neither showed how to dissolve it nor why it formed in the first place.

When I contemplated a flower or a tree under the influence of peyote, I perceived with perfect clarity that the verbal (logical) description of what was happening did not correspond at all to what was really happening.

Words were pure: tree was the name of the angel living in this part of the universe, but a shadow grew from their combination.

It would have been just as right—or just as wrong—to say that the tree was contemplating me, or even that contemplation was "treeing" me. (In the wonderful translation of *Le livre du commencement* [The Book of the Beginnings] that we owe to Edmund Fleg, God said, "When I will cloud in clouds above the world . . .").

I used to locate the consciousness in my mind, never asking myself if this place was legitimate, and I used to build my philosophical castles on the basis of this "obvious fact," on what I took to be the basis of this obvious fact. Why? It took me almost ten years to find an answer to this question.

The truth is quite simple, but it is inexpressible. One would need to invent a new grammar and a new logic to formulate it. At the moment, because it is impossible to formulate, we need to content ourselves with *expressing* it. This is what poets do.

A fundamental contradiction is indeed erased from the metaphor, the contradiction between the human and the inhuman. This contradiction is the mother of all contradictions, in a way, and, consequently, it is also the cause of all our mental distractions.

When Breton, for example, writes, "My wife whose hair is a brush fire," he shows us that opposition is an illusion, which means only verbal. (The poem "Free Union" is an illustration of this truth.) We tremble at the realization that this world is our world and that our world is also the other world. Then we are ready to hear the ancient philosopher Plotinus's sublime language:

> For all things in intelligible heaven are heaven. There the earth is heaven, just as the sea, animals, plants, and men are heaven. They perceive all things, not such indeed as are subject to generation. They likewise perceive themselves in others. For all things are there perfectly perspicuous. Nothing there is dark, nothing opposing, but everything is conspicuous to all, intrinsically and universally. For light everywhere meets with light. Each thing contains in itself all, and all things are again beheld in another. So that all things are everywhere, and all is all. There, everything is all. There, the sun is all the stars; and every star is a sun and at the same time all the stars. No one goes there, as if it was a foreign land.

INDEX

BOOKS OF RELATED INTEREST

DMT: The Spirit Molecule
A Doctor's Revolutionary Research into the Biology
of Near-Death and Mystical Experiences
by Rick Strassman, M.D.

The Psychedelic Explorer's Guide
Safe, Therapeutic, and Sacred Journeys
by James Fadiman, Ph.D.

Spiritual Growth with Entheogens
Psychoactive Sacramentals and Human Transformation
Edited by Thomas B. Roberts, Ph.D.

The New Science of Psychedelics
At the Nexus of Culture, Consciousness, and Spirituality
by David Jay Brown

Cactus of Mystery
The Shamanic Powers of the Peruvian San Pedro Cactus
by Ross Heaven

The Psilocybin Solution
The Role of Sacred Mushrooms in the Quest for Meaning
by Simon G. Powell

Timothy Leary: The Harvard Years
Early Writings on LSD and Psilocybin with Richard Alpert,
Huston Smith, Ralph Metzner, and others
Edited by James Penner

Plants of the Gods
Their Sacred, Healing, and Hallucinogenic Powers
by Richard Evans Schultes, Albert Hofmann, and Christian Rätsch

INNER TRADITIONS • BEAR & COMPANY
P.O. Box 388
Rochester, VT 05767
1-800-246-8648
www.InnerTraditions.com

Or contact your local bookseller